THE MASSACHUSETTS TOWN MEETING

A TENACIOUS INSTITUTION

THE MASSACHUSETTS TOWN MEETING
A TENACIOUS INSTITUTION

By Joseph F. Zimmerman

Professor of Political Science

Graduate School of Public Affairs

State University of New York at Albany

GRADUATE SCHOOL OF PUBLIC AFFAIRS

STATE UNIVERSITY OF NEW YORK AT ALBANY

ALBANY, NEW YORK

Printed in the United States of America
by Williams Press, Inc., Albany, New York

Foreword

The Graduate School of Public Affairs was established in 1962 by State University of New York to provide educational preparation for academic and public service careers, assist in the continuing professional development of government executives, and undertake research on significant public problems and issues. To make generally available such research by its faculty members, the Graduate School established a monograph series on public policy issues. This monograph is the fourth in the series.

O. B. CONAWAY, JR.
Dean

Preface

The Massachusetts open town meeting originated in the late 1620s and currently is found in two hundred seventy of the three hundred twelve towns; forty-two towns have abandoned the open town meeting in favor of the representative town meeting.

Criticism of town meeting government has been prevalent in the twentieth century, yet no town has become a city since 1922. The purposes of this monograph are to trace the origin of town meeting government, analyze the reasons for its tenacity, and evaluate how well it is meeting the challenges of the second half of the twentieth century.

For their many suggestions for the improvement of this monograph, I wish to acknowledge my indebtedness to the following: Dr. John Gillespie, Director of State Colleges in Massachusetts; Professor William G. O'Hare, Jr. of Salem State College; Mr. Robert J. M. O'Hare, Director of the Bureau of Public Affairs of Boston College; Mr. Elwyn E. Mariner, Research Director of the Massachusetts Taxpayers Foundation, Incorporated; and my colleague, Dr. Robert Rienow. The manuscript was typed by Miss Betty Jones.

Parts of this monograph have appeared previously in *Civic Affairs, The Massachusetts Selectman, National Civic Review,* and *Social Science.*

Albany, New York   J. F. Z.
November, 1966

Table of Contents

Chapter 1

Genesis of the Massachusetts Town

A proper understanding and appreciation of town government in Massachusetts cannot be achieved without reference to the past. Town government had its genesis in the late 1620s and made its appearance in recognizable form in the early 1630s.

Origin

The first English colony in New England was the Popham colony which was established on August 29, 1607 at the mouth of the Kennebec River and abandoned the following spring.[1] Prior to the landing of the Pilgrims at Plymouth, Massachusetts in 1620, fishing settlements existed along the coast but were not of the nature of permanent settlements and possessed no organized local government.[2] Relatively little is known about these settlements other than the fact they were temporary abodes of fishermen who maintained their permanent homes elsewhere.

The first permanent settlement of Massachusetts may be attributed in large measure to the bitter animosity which developed between the Church of England and two dissident groups: the Pilgrims and the Puritans who sought a more complete reformation of the Church of England.[3]

The Pilgrims originally were a small group of farmers and artisans of the lower and middle classes living in Scrooby, England who were called "Separatists" because they had separated from the Church of England and in the fall of 1606 formed their own church.[4] The Pilgrims believed that the reformation was incomplete and the Church of England retained too many features of the Church of Rome.

---

[1] *Tercentenary of the Landing of the Popham Colony at the Mouth of the Kennebec River, August, 29, 1907* (Portland: Maine Historical Society, 1907), pp. 2-28.

[2] Samuel G. Drake, *The History and Antiquities of Boston, from Its Settlement in 1630 to the year 1770* (Boston: Luther Stevens, 1856), p. 29.

[3] Francis S. Drake. *The Town of Roxbury* (Boston: Municipal Printing Office, 1905), p. 2.

[4] See Roland G. Usher. *The Pilgrams and Their History* (New York: The Macmillian Company, 1918).

Roland G. Usher maintained that the Pilgrims were not actively persecuted by the Church of England or the government, but by their neighbors.[5] The Pilgrims concluded that England was contaminated and a hazard to their spiritual welfare. In consequence, they decided in 1607 to emigrate to the Netherlands where they had heard freedom of religion existed for all. How many made the trip is not known but their community was established in Leyden in 1608.

Life in Leyden was hard for the Pilgrims whose lack of skills restricted them to the lowest paying positions. The fun loving Dutch by their light-hearted behavior on Sundays shocked the Pilgrims and the danger was ever present that the Pilgrims would be absorbed by the Dutch. By 1620, many Pilgrim children were speaking Dutch and several members of the church had become Dutch citizens; the Pilgrims feared their children might lack the dedication to resist the influence of Dutch society and the great reform movement might die. Consequently, a decision was made to emigrate to America and settle with the permission of the Virginia Company of London in Virginia where they could practice their religious beliefs freely without being molested by neighbors, and life would be easier and more conducive to the establishment of a utopian society. The Pilgrims journeyed to England and set sail from Plymouth on September 6, 1620.

The Pilgrims landed in Massachusetts which was outside the jurisdiction of the Virginia Company of London. The reasons for the landing in Massachusetts are not clear; adverse weather conditions may have been a factor. Of course, the possibility exists that the landing in Massachusetts may have been pre-determined by the Pilgrims because there was no established church in New England or for other reasons. The lack of a charter was remedied by the signing on November 11, 1620 of the Mayflower Compact which established the basis of government in the Colony.

The Mayflower Compact reads in part as follows:

> In the name of God Amen! We whose names are under written . . . do by these presents, solemnly and mutally, in the presence of God and one another covenant and combine ourselves together into a civil body politic for our better ordering and preservation, and furtherance of the ends aforesaid; and by virtue hereof to enact, constitute and frame just and equal laws, ordinances, acts, constitutions, and offices from time to time, as shall be thought most mete and convenient for the general good of the colony; unto which we promise all due submission and obedience . . .

[5] *Ibid.*, p. 17.

As the Plymouth Colony was never granted a royal charter it was governed by the Mayflower Compact until the Colony was merged with the Massachusetts Bay Colony in 1692. Fragmentary evidence available indicates that the leaders of the Plymouth Colony possessed complete power over the colonists and could refuse permission to new-comers to locate in the Colony unless they were considered to be prospective members of the church. The Pilgrims exhibited relatively little interest in political philosophy or institutions. Their apparent disinterest in government resulted from the great importance they attached to the doctrines of their church designed to promote their spiritual welfare.[6]

Relatively little is known of the early government of Plymouth Colony, but it is certain that its contribution to the development of the Massachusetts town was minor because Plymouth was directly ruled by the Governor and Council of the Colony and not allowed to develop as a direct democracy. With the exception of Scituate which in 1636 was authorized "to make such orders . . . for their convenient & comfortable living as they shall find necessary,"[7] Plymouth performed all governmental functions until 1651 when Sandwich was permitted to be governed by an elected board of selectmen who were authorized to call town meetings.[8]

In addition to the theocratic government established on the south shore, several fishing villages were established on the north shore but were of a temporary nature. An attempt was made by the Dorchester Company to establish at Cape Ann a permanent fishing base but it was abandoned in 1626; no civil government had been established at Cape Ann.[9]

While the Pilgrims were meeting in Scrooby there was in England a group of men who were not separatists but wished to reform the Church of England and "purify" its liturgy. The Puritans were men of wealth and station in England who were feeling the distress of the times including the political uncertainties resulting from the continuing struggles between the Crown and Parliament. The Puritans did

---

[6] Francis Baylies. *Historical Memoir of the Colony of New Plymouth* Vol. I. (Boston: Wiggin & Lunt, 1866), pp. 256-57.

[7] Nathaniel B. Shurtleff, (ed.), *Records of the Colony of New Plymouth in New England, Vol. I.* (Boston: From the Press of William White, Printer to the Commonwealth, 1855), p. 44.

[8] Henry C. Kittredge. *Barnstable: 1639-1939* (Barnstable, Massachusetts: Tercentenary Committee, 1939), p. 12.

[9] Clifford K. Shipton. *Roger Conant* (Cambridge: Harvard University Press, 1944), pp. 50-59.

not suffer persecution in England, yet concluded they had little chance of achieving victory in their campaign to reform the Church of England, and decided to emigrate to Massachusetts Bay. Although a number of writers have held that theology was responsible for the settlement of the Massachusetts Bay Colony, it would appear that the motivation was religious, economic and commercial.

Charles I granted the royal charter of the Massachusetts Bay Company, a joint stock company, which created "one body politique and corporate in fact and name, by the name of the Governor and company of the Massachusetts Bay in New England." [10] The charter, which passed the seals on March 4, 1628-9,[11] provided for a Governor, Deputy Governor, and eighteen Assistants who were authorized to hold a General Court, to admit freemen, to elect officers, and make laws governing the inhabitants of the Colony.[12]

The charter was similar to charters possessed by other commercial and trading companies of its day and this has led some to conclude that the motivation for the foundation of the Company was principally commercial. Yet the charter contained the following statement which bespeaks its theological purpose: The charter authorizes the General Court to make orders, laws, and statutes "whereby our said people inhabitants there, maie be soe religiously, peaceablie, and civilly governed, as their good life and orderlie coversacon maie wynn and incite the natives of the country to the knowledg and obedience of the onlie true God and Savior of mankinde, and the Christian fayth, which, in our royall intercon and the adventureers free profession, is the principall ende of this plantacon." [13]

The Puritans brought to Massachusetts Bay a carefully conceived concept of an ideal society and a plan for its future development. This concept included political and economic institutions borrowed from England and adapted to the exigencies of life in Massachusetts Bay.[14]

The records of the Massachusetts Bay Company unfortunately are not as complete as desired by scholars. The first few entries deal pri-

---

[10] Nathaniel B. Shurtleff, (ed.), *Records of the Governor and Company of the Massachusetts Bay in New England,* Vol. I. (Boston: From the Press of William White, Printer to the Commonwealth, 1853), p. 10.

[11] The Julian calendar was in use at the time and the year legally commenced on March 25th. The first date in a double date refers to the legal year and the second date to the historical year.

[12] Shurtleff, *Records of the Governor and Company* I, pp. 10-17.

[13] *Ibid.,* p. 17.

[14] William Haller, Jr. *The Puritan Town-Planting in New England Colonial Development 1630-1660* (New York: Columbia University Press, 1951), p. 13.

marily with securing supplies for the plantation and authorizing Governor John Endicott and Council to make necessary laws and orders for the governing of the plantation. It appears the Puritans felt their new commonwealth could be successful only if the government was controlled by the colonists. If the stockholders resided in England, they might be pressured by the Crown to adopt policies injurious to the new colony and the danger existed that control of a majority of the stock of the company might fall into the hands of persons unsympathetic to the noble purposes of the Puritans. John Winthrop and others planning to migrate to Massachusetts Bay purchased the shares of those who desired to remain in England. On May 22, 1629, the question of transferring the government to New England was raised for the first time and on August 29, 1629 the transfer was voted.[15] The form of government for the new Colony was established at the third meeting of the General Court in the new world when it voted on October 19, 1630 to authorize freemen to choose Assistants and the Assistants were authorized to elect from among themselves a Governor and Deputy Governor who with the Assistants would have the power to enact laws and select officers to execute the laws.[16]

Sites for towns were selected on the basis of available springs and defensibility against Indian attack. The territorial area of the town was small and was determined primarily by the convenience of getting to the Sunday meeting as attendance was compulsory and absence was subject to a fine or other penalty.[17] The General Court on September 2, 1635 ordered that no dwelling house could be built more than one-half mile beyond the meeting house in any new plantation without the permission of the Court.[18] As the houses were clustered close together around the common and the meeting house, the individual lots were necessarily small and each lot contained enough space for a house, small outbuildings, and a small garden. Land suitable for cultivation near the center of the town was divided among the settlers in an equitable manner. Each man was responsible for keeping his fields "sufficiently fenced" and town meetings appointed individuals to see that fields were adequately fenced. The penalty in Dorchester

---

[15] Shurtleff, *Records of the Governor and Company* I, pp. 49 and 51.

[16] *Ibid.,* p. 79.

[17] James K. Hosmer. *Samuel Adams, The Man of the Town Meeting* (Baltimore: John Hopkins University Studies in Historical and Political Science, Vol. II., No. IV, 1884), pp. 8-9.

[18] Shurtleff, *Records of the Governor and Company* I, p. 157.

for failing to fence properly a field was three shillings.[19] The common land situated near the extremities of the town was used at first for pasture and a source of wood, but was later distributed to new settlers.[20]

The completeness of the early records in the towns varied considerably. In general, the early records are sketchy and provide only a rough picture of town government. Yet they indicate considerable diversity in governmental practices in the various towns. Consequently, it is difficult to arrive at generalizations that are valid for all early towns.

The Folkmoot

The charter of the Plymouth Company, the Mayflower Compact, and the charter of the Massachusetts Bay Company did not contemplate town government and, consequently, made no reference to towns or their government.

The first towns in the Massachusetts Bay Colony were governed by a folkmoot or an extra-legal and informal assemblage of the freemen. All matters affecting the welfare of the town such as the division of land, building of a church, hiring of a minister, and admission of new inhabitants were discussed and decisions made. Attendance at town meetings was compulsory; absences were punished by a fine and early records contain the names of citizens who failed to attend the town meeting. No town officials were elected during the earliest stage of the development of the New England town form of government. Town government at this stage had not become institutionalized and was completely informal. No town charters existed, no permanent organization was established, the number and frequency of meetings was indeterminate, and no specific duties had been established for the town meeting or town officials as they began to make their appearance.

The distinguishing characteristic of the first New England towns was the primary assembly of the citizens as the ruling body. This was "pure" democracy in action and remains as a distinguishing characteristic in two hundred and seventy of the three hundred and twelve Massachusetts towns.

---

[19] Boston, Massachusetts, *Dorchester Town Records.* Fourth Report of the Record Commissioners of the City of Boston. 2nd ed. (Boston: Rockwell and Churchill, 1883), p. 3.

[20] George L. Haskins. *Law and Authority in Early Massachusetts* (New York: The Macmillan Company, 1960), pp. 69-70.

The primary assembly in the beginning in some towns was held weekly but soon gave way to a monthly meeting. Cambridge at a meeting held on December 24, 1632 established the policy of monthly meetings.[21] During the year 1635 meetings were held in Boston on the following dates: January 23, February 13, September 30, October 4, October 14, November 4, November 23, and December 19. Six meetings were held in Boston during the year 1698.[22] In 1663, Watertown decided to hold an annual town meeting on the first Monday of September.[23]

The actual practice at the early town meetings was not adequately documented and undoubtedly varied from town to town. It appears that all male residents of the town generally were permitted to attend town meetings and speak. However, only freemen usually were allowed to vote. Freemen originally were the shareholders of the Massachusetts Bay Company and later included men who were granted political freedom. An entry in the Company records dated October 19, 1630 contains the names of one hundred and ten men who desired to be made freemen, but fails to mention if any action was taken.[24] The General Court on May 18, 1631 voted that men could not be admitted as freemen "of this body polliticke" unless they were "members of some of the churches within the lymitts of the same."[25] On March 3, 1636, the General Court ordered no person shall be admitted as a freeman if he is a member of a church which was organized without the approbation of the magistrates and a majority of the existing churches.[26] On May 18, 1631, one hundred and sixteen men took the oath of freemen and between March 6, 1632 and March 4, 1636 three hundred and forty men took the oath of freemen.[27] Available evidence indicates that freemen constituted a very small percentage of the adult male population in the Massachusetts Bay Colony.[28]

[21] Cambridge, Massachusetts, *The Records of the Town of Cambridge (Formerly Newtowne) Massachusetts 1630-1703* (Cambridge: Printed by order of the City Council under direction of the City Clerk, 1901), p. 4.

[22] Boston, Massachusetts, *Second Report of the Record Commissioners of the City of Boston* (Boston: Rockwell and Churchill, 1877), pp. 2-9 and 222-40.

[23] Watertown, Massachusetts, *Watertown Records* (Watertown: Press of Fred G. Barker, 1894), p. 78.

[24] Shurtleff, *Records of the Governor and Company* I, pp. 78-80.

[25] *Ibid.*, p. 87.

[26] *Ibid.*, p. 168.

[27] *Ibid.*, pp. 367-70.

[28] Haller, *Puritan Town-Planting,* p. 22.

On April 1, 1634, the General Court required every male over twenty years of age who had lived in the Colony and was not a freeman to take an oath acknowledging he and his family were subject to the government of Massachusetts and would be obedient to the magistrates and all laws enacted. Furthermore, he was required to pledge to notify the authorities if he heard of any sedition, violence, or treachery being plotted against the government.[29] If any man twice refused to take the oath, he was banished from the Colony unless the Court granted him a respite.

The General Court on May 14, 1634 voted to require freemen to take the following oath which grew out of experimentation with earlier oaths.

> I, A. B., being, by Gods providence, an inhabitant & ffreeman within the jurisdiction of this comonweale, doe freely acknowledge my selfe to be subject to the goverm^t thereof & therefore doe heere sweare, by the greate & dreadfull name of the euerlyveing God, that I will be true & faithful to the same, & will accordingly yielde assistance & support therevnto, . . . submitting my selfe to the wholesome lawes & orders made & established by the same; and furth^r, that I will not plott nor practice any euill against it, nor consent to any that soe doe, but will timely discover & reveale the same to lawful aucthority nowe here established, for the speedy preventing thereof . . . I will giue my vote & suffrage, as I shall iudge im myne owne conscience may best conduce & tend to the publique weale of the body, without respect of psons, or fav^r of any man. Soe helpe mee God, in the Lord Jesus Christ.[30]

The early towns were ethnocentric in character and their records contain numerous reference to the admission of individuals to towns and the treatment of "strangers" by the citizens of a town. In some towns the town meeting empowered the selectmen to admit men as "townsmen." The town frequently would require a newcomer to find a sponsor among the town's residents or post a bond guaranteeing that he would not become a poor relief burden to the town. The *Dorchester Records* contain an interesting reference to the receiving of strangers in the town in 1658.

> Not to p'vent such inconuenience as may come if euery one be at liberty to receiue into this towne whom they please. It is ordered therefore by the select men of this towne that if any maner of p'son ore p'sons in this towne shall intertaine anyh soiorour ore inmate into his or ther house ore habitation aboue one weeke without lisence from the selectmen ore the maior parte of them first had and obtained, shall forfeit fiue shillings, and for every weekes Continuance three shillings foure pence.[31]

---

[29] Shurtleff, *Records of the Governor and Company,* I, pp. 115-16.
[30] *Ibid.,* p. 117.
[31] *Dorchester Records,* p. 95.

8

The Dorchester Records also report that in 1662 ". . . Daniel Eliers came to the select men and intreated to be an inhabitant in Dorchester; the selectmen would not accept of him to be an inhabitant unless he did bring a sufficient man or men to be bound to secure the towne of him, or to be in couenant for one yeare with some honest man."[32]

Foreigners coming into Watertown had no rights "either of Commonage, or land vndivided" but were authorized to buy an inhabitant's rights.[33] During the late 1600s fewer references to strangers or land disposition appear in the official records of the towns.

It appears that many early town meetings were lively affairs and in some instances disorderly. The following entry in the *Dorchester Records* dated "The 18 of the 10 month 1642" is of considerable interest.

> Whereas it hath beene obserued diuerse tymes, in our general Towne meetings, that some Confusion and disorder hath happened in the agitation of our publicke matters and plantation affaires, by reason that men haue used thire libertye to p'pound theer matters to the Plantation without any fore knoledge of the seauen men, and theere matters have been so followed that diuerse things haue beene spoken of and few matters haue beene issued by reason that new matters haue been vpsterted and lytle worke don, and moreouer the spirits of som men trobled and offended by reason that thire matters could not be hearde, it is thearefore ordered by the 7 men that al matters and questions which any man hath agitated and petions to be answered by the Plantation shall first be brought to the 7 men or to some tow or more of them, and by them Consydered and orderly p^r sented to the plantation who shal follow the busines, together with the Plantation, without any interruption, by any matters incerted, to the Conclusion and determynation theareof, except it be vnreasonably refused by the 7 men otherwyse euery person ofending against this order shal forfeyt for the same syx pence for euery such offenc to be leuyed by distresse for the use of the towne.[34]

Emergence of Town Officials

The town meeting soon proved inadequate for the governing of town affairs and town officials began to appear. With their appearance town meetings were held with less frequency and often only once a year to elect officers and conduct town business; special meetings were held if needed.

The first town official to appear in the records of the Massachusetts Bay Company was the constable. The Court of Assistants on Septem-

---

[32] *Ibid.*, pp. 113-14.
[33] *Watertown Records*, p. 2.
[34] *Dorchester Records*, pp. 50-51.

ber 28, 1630 appointed the constables of Salem and Dorchester.[35] On October 19, 1630, the General Court appointed the constable in Charlton, Rocksbury, and Watertown.[36] The constable undoubtedly was considered the most important town official in the early days of the town as he was selected by the General Court and was the only town official referred to in the records of the Company until April 1, 1634 when the General Court ordered the constable and four or more "of the cheife inhabitants" of every town to survey the houses, corn fields, and other lands, and enter their findings in a book, a copy of which was to be transmitted to the General Court.[37] He warned the inhabitants of all town meetings and also acted as the tax collector in smaller towns.

The first locally elected town officials to make their appearance in the early town records were the selectmen. The *Dorchester Records* first refer to them on October 8, 1633.[38] Terms of office usually were either annual or semi-annual.

The Massachusetts town started off with a plural executive: the selectmen. During the early years of town government selectmen were not called by their present title but were called "townsmen" in Cambridge,[39] "selected townsmen," "the seven," the "nine" men or "Chosen men for managing the prudential affairs," and in Dorchester "The names of such as were chosen for the ordering of the affares of the plantation."[40] An entry dated "This 24th of the 1st mo., 1642" in the *Boston Records* contains the first reference to the term "selectmen."[41] An entry in the *Cambridge Records* dated November 20, 1665 is entitled "At a meeting of the Selectmen" but refers to "The Townsmen" issuing orders.[42]

The number of selectmen varied from town to town and from time to time within a town: the range being from three in Charlestown to twelve in Dorchester. The October 8, 1633 town meeting of Dorchester agreed that there should be twelve selectmen but the following year on October 28th the town meeting decided that there should be ten selectmen.[43] The selectmen frequently met in the home of one of their

[35] Shurtleff, *Records of the Governor and Company* I, p. 76.
[36] *Ibid.*, p. 79.
[37] *Ibid.*, p. 116.
[38] *Dorchester Records*, p. 3.
[39] *Cambridge Records*, p. 50.
[40] *Dorchester Records*, p. 19.
[41] *Boston Records*, p. 68.
[42] *Cambridge Records*, p. 159.
[43] *Dorchester Records*, pp. 3 and 7.

members and the clerk recorded their proceedings in the same book in which he recorded the proceedings of the town meetings.

The duties assigned the selectmen by the town meeting differed to some extent from town to town. In Watertown their duties included the division of town lands, repairing and enlarging the meeting house, surveying the inhabitants relative to their knowledge of God, and ensuring that children received an education.[44] In Dorchester their duties included regulating the presence of strangers in the town, laying out ways, appointing a captain and lieutenant to be in charge of the ammunition, regulating the sale of cider and the cutting of trees, and selecting a schoolmaster.[45] Selectmen in the early days also performed certain judicial functions.[46] Decisions could be made by a majority of the selectmen present provided there was a quorum. In Dorchester in 1634 there were ten selectmen and a quorum of seven was established.[47] The town meeting, however, kept ultimate power in its own hands and the selectmen acted principally as an executive committee of the town meeting.

The *Dorchester Records* contain a curious document referred to as "The Directory" which gives charges to the selectmen.

> Fourthly we require that our 7 men shalbe careffull to meet 8 tymes in the yeare viz the 2 mondaye of euery month in the yeare except the 2:5:6:8 at some place which shal be certainly knowne vnto all the Tow and there to be Resident from 9 oclocke in the aff ore noone vnto 3 oclocke in the afternoone: that so all such haue any Complaints or Requests to make or any information to giue or anything what soeuer to doe with them moie Certainely Find all or 5 of them at the Least.[48]

One of the seven selectmen in Dorchester was appointed the moderator because of "intemperate Clashings in our Towne meetings."[49]

The most complete early record describing the government of a Massachusetts town is contained in the report of the town meeting held in Dorchester on October 8, 1633.

> *Inprimus* it is ordered that for the generall good and well ordering of the affayres of the Plantation their shall be every Mooneday before the Court by eight of the Clocke in the morning, and p^r sently upon the beating of the drum, a generall meeting of the inhabitants of the Plantation att the meeteing house, there to settle (and sett downe) such orders as may tend to the generall good as aforesays: and every man to be bound

---

[44] *Watertown Records,* p. 2.
[45] *Dorchester Records,* pp. 95, 99, 110, 177, and 257.
[46] *Boston Records,* pp. 97 and 112.
[47] *Dorchester Records,* p. 7.
[48] *Ibid.,* p. 290.
[49] *Ibid.,* pp. 292-93.

thereby without gaynesaying or resistance. It is also agreed that there shall be twelve men selected out of the Company that may or the greatest p't of them meete as aforesayd to determine as aforesayd, yet so as it is desired that the most of the Plantation will keepe the meeteing constantly and all that are there although none of the Twelve shall have a free voyce as any of the 12 and that the great(r) vote both of the 12 and the other shall be of force and efficasy and aforesayd. And it is likewise ordered that all things concluded as aforesay shall stand in force and be obeyed untill the next monethly meeteing and aferwardes if it not contradicted and otherwise ordered upon the sayd monethly meete (ing) by the greatest p'te of those that are pʳ sent as aforesayd:[50]

Although the selectmen were the first elected officials mentioned in early town records, the existence of the records is conclusive evidence that someone was charged with the duty of keeping them. In 1656, *Dorchester Records* refer to the choice of a "recorder" for the town[51] and the *Boston Records* under an entry dated "12 March 9/23" refer to the "Towne Clarke."[52] The functions of the town clerk in many respects were similar to those of the vestry clerk in England.

Not only was attendance at town meetings compulsory, but office holding was compulsory for those elected. The records of the October 28, 1634 town meeting in Dorchester contain the following entry. "It is agreed that whosoever is chosen in to any office for the good of the Plantation, he shall abide by it, or submit to a fine as the company shall thinke meete to impose."[53] In Boston in 1653 "Joseph Rock was fined twenty shillings for refusing to accept the office of a Constable, being legally chosen thereunto."[54]

Theories of Origin

A considerable dispute raged among historians during the latter quarter of the nineteenth century over the question of the origin of the Massachusetts town. It was held that the Massachusetts town was (1) indigenous in origin; (2) a lineal descendent of the ancient Anglosaxon *tun;* and (3) an adaptation to a new environment of English institutions with which the colonists were familiar.

The first theory is a parthenogenetic one which held that the Massachusetts town developed spontaneously as a new political institution

---

[50] *Ibid.,* p. 3.
[51] *Ibid.,* p. 83.
[52] *Boston Records,* p. 212.
[53] *Dorchester Records,* p. 8.
[54] *Boston Records,* p. 115.

on the rocky shores of Massachusetts as the colonists faced an environment completely foreign to them. Evidence to support this theory is completely lacking.

Herbert B. Adams held that the Massachusetts towns were descendants of English local institutions which in turn had descended from Germanic prototypes. Writing in 1882 he reported that the villages in southern Germany were physically similar to New England rural towns.[55] Adams came to the conclusion that the New England town meeting grew out of the primordial field meetings of German farmers held for the purpose of distributing land and regulating crops; the village elders were the forerunners of the constable and selectmen of the Massachusetts town.[56] Adams wrote:

> The original idea of New England Towns, like that of their Old English and Germanic prototypes, was that of a village community of allied families, settled in close proximity for good neighborhood and defense, with homes and home lots fenced in and owned in severalty, but with a common Town Street and a Village Green or Home Pasture, and with common fields, alloted outside the Town for individual mowing and tillage but fenced in common, together with a vast surrounding tract of absolutely common and undivided land, used for pasture and woodland under communal regulations.[57]

Whether a lineage can be established descending from the ancient Germanic *tuns* through Anglo-Saxon institutions to the New England town is debatable. Certainly the similarities between the New England town and the Germanic *tun* may be partially or completely coincidental rather than evolutionary. The records of the early Massachusetts towns are fragmentary regarding the origin of the town form of government, but contain nothing to suggest a conscious copying of Germanic institutions.

The third theory held that the colonists upon their arrival in Massachusetts adapted the English manor and vestry with which they were familiar to a totally new situation. Many similarities exist between the New England town and older English institutions which suggests a continuity between them. In England, prior to the settlement of colonies in Massachusetts, parishioners met in the vestry to make decisions concerning the support of the church and elected churchwardens who

---

[55] Herbert B. Adams, *The Germanic Origin of New England Towns* (Baltimore: Johns Hopkins University Studies in Historical and Political Science, Vol. I, No. II, 1882), p. 12.

[56] *Ibid.,* p. 18.

[57] *Ibid.,* pp. 27-28.

were placed in charge of the property of the church.[58] Following the break with the Church of Rome, laws were passed imposing many civil duties upon the churchwardens including the hiring of schoolmasters and the administering of laws. The vestry meeting and the churchwardens correspond in certain respects to the town meeting and the selectmen respectively.

Support for the third theory is found in the records of the Court of Assistants held at Charlestown on August 23, 1630; the Court stipulated that justices of the peace shall have "like power that justices of the peace hath in England." [59] Further evidence is the fact that churchwardens in England were referred to in the records as "the four," "the twelve," or "the sixteen" [60] and selectmen in the early Massachusetts towns were referred to as "the ten" and the "seven men." [61]

Sumner C. Powell's recent study of the settlement of Sudbury, Massachusetts has shattered a number of generalizations about the early Massachusetts towns.[62] Powell points out that the settlers of Sudbury did not emigrate from the same English village, but rather from a large number of boroughs, parishes, and towns.[63] The early Sudbury leaders evidently borrowed from each of these systems of local government in constructing the governmental system in Sudbury. Powell reached the conclusion "there were multiple origins and many distinct early towns, and that all of these towns and their relationships need careful examination.[64]

Available evidence supports the theory that the settlers in each town adapted a number of familiar English institutions to the exigencies of life in Massachusetts Bay. It is not unreasonable to conclude that town institutions were forged by experimentation over a period of years.

---

[58] W. Eric Jackson, *Local Government in England and Wales* (Hardmonsworth, Middlesex: Penguin Books, Ltd., 1959), pp. 23-25, and Wallace Notestein, *The English People on the Eve of Colonization* (New York: Harper & Row, Publishers, 1954), pp. 240-49.

[59] Shurtleff, *Records,* I, p. 74.

[60] Notestein, *The English People,* p. 241.

[61] *Dorchester Records,* pp. 7 and 47.

[62] Sumner C. Powell. *Puritan Village* (Middletown, Connecticut: Wesleyan University Press, 1963).

[63] *Ibid.,* p. 6.

[64] *Ibid.,* p. 139.

Chapter 2

The Open Town Meeting

The town meeting is the distinguishing feature of town government in Massachusetts and is sanctioned by the Constitution of the Commonwealth adopted in 1780.

> The people have a right, in an orderly and peaceable manner, to assemble to consult upon the common good; give instructions to their representatives, and to request of the legislative body, by way of addresses, petitions, or remonstrances, redress of the wrongs done them, and of the grievances they suffer.[1]

The open town meeting, which developed as a primary assembly of freemen during the 1630s, remains fundamentally the same today as the local law making body in two hundred and seventy of the three hundred and twelve towns; its trappings have changed little. The development of the finance committee as a valuable adjunct to the town meeting represents the most important change in the town meeting structure in these towns.

The Annual Town Meeting

Somnolent appearing towns spring to life at annual town meeting time when town officials are elected and town business is transacted. Each town must hold its annual meeting in February, March, or April unless a special law specifies a different month; the selectmen may call special meetings when necessary.[2] Walpole, for example, holds its annual town meeting on the third Monday of January.[3] Meetings may be held any place in the town and adjourned when necessary. Traditionally town meetings have been held in the town hall, but the growth of towns has necessitated the use of larger assembly halls such as a school auditorium or gymnasium. The Attorney General of the Commonwealth has ruled that a town meeting may not be held in a regional school unless it is located in the town.[4] Ashburnham desired

---

[1] *Constitution of the Commonwealth of Massachusetts,* Part the First, art. XIX.

[2] *Massachusetts General Laws,* chap. 39, sec. 9.

[3] *Massachusetts Acts of 1924,* chap. 377, sec. 1.

[4] Commonwealth of Massachusetts, *Opinion of Edward J. McCormack, Attorney General,* July 17, 1961.

to hold town meetings in the Oakmont Regional High School auditorium, but was prevented from so doing as the auditorium is located on the Westminster side of the building "which straddles the boundary between the two towns forming the district."[5]

Town meetings normally are called by the selectmen, but may be called by the town clerk if all the selectmen vacate their offices for any reason. If there is no town clerk, a justice of the peace may call a town meeting.[6] Should the selectmen unreasonably refuse to call a meeting, one hundred or ten per cent of the registered voters may submit a written application to a justice of the peace who is authorized to call a meeting by issuing a warrant.[7]

The Warrant

Each town meeting is held in pursuance of a warrant or warning which is the foundation stone of the town meeting as it contains a listing of the articles for consideration by the town meeting. The warrant is drafted by the selectmen who must give at least seven days notice when calling a town meeting.[8]

Since early towns were small and freemen were required subject to a fine to attend all town meetings, there was no need to prepare a warrant listing the articles to be considered. With the dropping of the compulsory attendance requirement and the growth of towns it became necessary to warn the voters of the matters to be considered at a town meeting in order to enable all voters interested in any or all matters to attend. The warrant is the most widely read publication in a town and may exceed in popularity the current best sellers.

It is not uncommon for the selectmen to list the more controversial articles first in the warrant for consideration early in the evening when attendance is at its peak; routine articles sometimes are rushed over near the end of the evening after many voters have left the meeting. This practice clearly is superior to the listing of polemical articles near the end of the warrant. The town meeting, however, may vote to consider articles out of the order in which they appear in the warrant.

---

[5] Commonwealth of Massachusetts, *Report Submitted by the Legislative Research Council Relative to Town Meetings in Regional Schools* (Boston: December 27, 1961), p. 18.

[6] *Massachusetts General Laws,* chap. 39, sec. 11.

[7] *Ibid.,* chap. 39, sec. 12.

[8] *Ibid.,* chap. 39, sec. 10.

A town meeting is not legal unless it is held in pursuance of a warrant issued by a majority of the selectmen, the town clerk, or a justice of the peace.[9] Only articles included in the warrant may be considered by the town meeting; in other words, the warrant is the fixed agenda for the town meeting and irrelevant motions may not be introduced.[10] The town meeting is not a continuing body as it is dissolved upon the completion of action on the warrant; the meeting cannot be reconvened. However, a new town meeting can be called into existence by a new warrant.

The selectmen may include in the warrant any article they wish to have considered by the town meeting and usually include articles requested by various town officers, boards, commissions, and committees. If there is no finance committee, the selectmen must prepare and submit the town budget to the annual town meeting.[11] The initiative may be used by the voters in every town to insert articles in the warrant. The General Court on December 22, 1715 first authorized the use of the initiative in towns by requiring the selectmen to insert in the warrant for calling a town meeting any matter accompanied by a petition signed by ten or more freeholders.[12] Selectmen must insert in the annual meeting warrant all articles they have been requested to insert in writing by ten or more registered voters prior to the closing of the warrant and in a special town meeting warrant all articles they have been requested to insert "in writing by one hundred registered voters or by ten per cent of the total number of registered voters of the town whichever number is the lesser."[13] However, the initiative is seldom used in most towns as the selectmen customarily include in the warrant any article requested verbally or in writing by a registered voter. In most instances the selectmen include a requested article as worded by the voter(s) even though the wording may be improper. Should the selectmen agree with the substance of the improperly worded article, they may insert a properly worded article immediately preceding the requested article; the adoption of the selectmen's article obviates the necessity of acting upon the following article and it usually is "passed over."

---

[9] *Reynolds v. Inhabitants of New Salem,* 47 Mass. 340 (1843).

[10] *Massachusetts General Laws,* chap. 39, sec. 10.

[11] *Ibid.,* chap. 39, sec. 16.

[12] *The Acts and Resolves of the Province of the Massachusetts Bay,* Vol. II (Boston: Wright and Potter, 1874), p. 30.

[13] *Massachusetts General Laws,* chap. 39, sec. 10.

The Supreme Judicial Court has ruled that "the object of a warrant is to give previous notice to the inhabitants of the subjects to be acted on, and if this is done substantially it is sufficient." [14] The Court later held "warrants for town meetings are not to be construed with technical precision; it is enough if they give intelligible notice of the subjects to be acted on at the meeting." [15] A warrant article "to hear the report of any committee heretofore chosen, and pass any vote in relation to the same" is adequate notice for a town meeting to vote funds recommended by a committee appointed at a previous town meeting under the provisions of a warrant which fully specified the business to be considered.[16] The Supreme Judicial Court also has ruled that an article in the warrant "to raise such sums as may be necessary to defray town charges for the ensuing year" is sufficient notice to allow the town meeting to vote to raise funds for specific town purposes.[17] An article in the warrant for a Williamstown annual meeting "to elect all necessary town officers for the ensuing year" was held to be sufficient notice to authorize the town meeting to invest the collector of taxes "with all the powers which a town treasurer has when appointed collector of taxes." [18] At an adjourned session of a town meeting any article in the warrant may be reconsidered provided the rights of other parties have not become vested under the votes passed at an earlier session.[19]

The procedure for notifying and warning the town of a forthcoming town meeting is formalized in law and tradition. The selectmen direct the warrant to the constables or other specified persons who give notice of the town meeting and make the return of the accomplishment of the directive according to the procedure specified in the town by-laws. In towns which lack by-laws, notice is given in the manner prescribed by a vote of the town meeting or the Attorney General of the Commonwealth.[20] In Oak Bluffs, for example, "all Town Meetings, including the annual meeting, shall be notified by posting notice thereof in two or more public places in the Town at least seven days before the time of said meeting, and by publishing the same in some newspaper published in the county. Such

---

[14] *Torrey v. The Inhabitants of Millbury,* 38 Mass. 64 (1838).

[15] *Kittredge v. Inhabitants of North Brookfield,* 138 Mass. 286 (1885).

[16] *Fuller v. Inhabitants of Groton,* 77 Mass. 340 (1858).

[17] *Westhampton v. Searle,* 127 Mass. 502 (1879).

[18] *Sherman v. Torrey,* 99 Mass. 472 (1868).

[19] *Reed v. Inhabitants of Acton,* 117 Mass. 384 (1875).

[20] *Massachusetts General Laws,* chap. 39, sec. 10.

notices shall contain the warrant in full which is to be acted upon in said meeting."[21] The return of a constable upon the warrant for a town meeting certifying he posted the warrant according to law without specifying the manner of posting is sufficient.[22] The Supreme Judicial Court has ruled that a by-law specifying that notice of a town meeting be posted at the town hall was complied with by posting the notice at the building where the meeting was to be held in view of the fact the town hall had been destroyed by fire.[23]

The Annual Report

The selectmen are required by general law subject to a fifty dollar fine to print, prior to the annual town meeting, the annual town report for the previous year containing the reports of town officers and boards, the jury list, and other matters required by law or town by-law to be included.[24] A copy must be sent to the State Library; failure to do so results in the Commonwealth withholding from the town publications which are distributed to other towns.[25] Although the selectmen must print the annual town report, they do not have to prepare it. In Adams the annual report is compiled and edited by the Permanent Town Report Committee authorized by a special town meeting held on June 24, 1963.

Several towns print the warrant for the forthcoming annual meeting in the annual report which contains the action taken on the articles in the warrant for the previous year's annual meeting and warrant for special town meetings, if any. This is a very desirable practice as it facilitates reference to previous action taken on warrant articles and pertinent information bearing on the articles contained in the reports of various town officials and boards.

Annual town reports often are difficult to read. Careful preparation and editing are prerequisites to the publication of readable annual reports. They should be written in a semi-popular style or contain a summary that is easy to read. Generous use should be made of charts, tables, maps, photographs, cartoons, and colors within the limits of reasonable cost. The 1964 Berlin annual report not only makes use of bar and pie charts, but also contains definitions of terms such as

[21] Oak Bluffs, Massachusetts, *By-Laws of the Town of Oak Bluffs, Massachusetts,* chap. III, sec. I.
[22] *Rand v. Wilder,* 65 Mass. 294 (1853).
[23] *Commonwealth v. Sullivan,* 165 Mass. 183 (1896).
[24] *Massachusetts General Laws,* chap. 40, sec. 49.
[25] *Ibid., chap.* 40, sec. 50.

"overlay," "free cash," and "cherry sheet" which are confusing to the average townsman.[26] One of the most effective types of annual reports is the report issued as a newspaper supplement. It generally is written with an unusual clarity of expression and is distributed to nearly every home in the town.

In an effort to improve town reports the Massachusetts Selectmen's Association sponsors an annual town report contest and presents awards for the best town report in each of six population classes.

Election of Town Officials

In the early towns, officials were elected first and business was conducted immediately following the elections. Terms of office were indeterminate, but generally were short ranging from a few months to one year. Various methods of voting were utilized at early town meetings. The General Court first regulated the manner of voting in town elections on November 11, 1647 when it ordered that voting shall be done by "beanes and paper."[27]

The General Court on November 16, 1692 passed the first act which generally regulated the election of town officers.[28] The annual town meeting for the election of officers was required to be held in March. Three, five, seven, or nine men were to be elected as selectmen and overseers of the poor; a town clerk, "a commissioner for assessments, constables, surveyors of highways, tythingmen, fence-viewers, clerks of the market, sealers of leather, and other ordinary town officers" also were to be elected. On January 15, 1743, the General Court passed an act stipulating that no person could participate in the election of officers and the conduct of business at a town meeting unless he was "personally present at such meeting, and have a rateable estate in such town . . . besides the poll, amounting to the value of twenty pounds."[29]

Although one year terms for town officials are common today, the trend is toward longer terms. With certain exceptions, towns presently

---

[26] Berlin, Massachusetts, *Annual Report of the Several Official Boards of the Town of Berlin, Massachusetts,* 1964, pp. 5 and 144-45.

[27] Nathaniel B. Shurtleff, (ed.), *Records of the Governor and Company of the Massachusetts Bay in New England,* Vol. II (Boston: From the Press of William White, Printer to the Commonwealth, 1853), p. 220.

[28] *The Acts and Resolves, Public and Private of the Province of the Massachusetts Bay,* Vol. I (Boston: Wright and Potter, 1869), p. 65.

[29] *The Acts and Resolves of the Province of the Massachusetts Bay,* Vol. III (Boston: Wright and Potter, 1869), p. 47.

are required at the annual meeting when the term of any official expires to elect by ballot from among the registered voters a town clerk for one or more years; a town treasurer for a one or three year term; one or more collectors of taxes for a one or three year term unless the town meeting votes to have the treasurer act as collector; three or five selectmen for a one or three year term; one, three or five assessors for three year terms; three or five members of a board of public welfare unless the town meeting authorizes the selectmen to act as a board of welfare; one or three auditors for a term of one or three years; one or more highway surveyors for a one or three year term; a road commissioner and a sewer commissioner for a one year term or three road commissioners and three sewer commissioners for three year terms unless the town meeting authorizes the road commissioners to act as sewer commissioners; a tree warden for a one or three year term; one or more constables for three year terms unless the town meeting votes they shall be appointed; three, five, six, seven, or nine members of the school committee for three year terms; and three members of the board of health for three year terms unless the selectmen act as the board of health.[30]

The decisions relative to the terms and number of town officials and consolidations of offices are not made at each annual meeting. The town officials to be elected at a given annual meeting and their terms have been determined at previous town meetings. "In any case where three or more members of a board are to be elected for terms of more than one year, as nearly one third as may be shall be elected annually." [31] Failure to elect selectmen or assessors subjects the town to a fine of one to five hundred dollars as the county commissioners determine.[32]

The warrant for the annual town meeting warns the voters of the forthcoming election of town officers as well as the business to be considered. For example, the warrant for the 1964 Templeton annual town meeting reads in part as follows:

> In the name of the Commonwealth of Massachusetts, you are directed to notify and warn the inhabitants of each of the several precincts of the Town of Templeton, County of Worcester, qualified to vote in Elections and Town places designated and appointed, by the Selectmen, to wit:
> In Precinct No. 1 — First Church Chapel Hall
> In Precinct No. 2 — Scout Hall
> In Precinct No. 3 — Otter River School

[30] *Massachusetts General Laws,* chap. 41, sec. 1.
[31] *Ibid.*
[32] Ibid., chap. 41, sec. 4.

In Precinct No. 4 — American Legion Hall
on Monday the second day of March, next, at 11 o'clock A. M.
to bring in their votes to the election officers, on one ballot . . .
The Polls will open at 11 o'clock A. M. and be closed at 7
o'clock P. M. And you are further directed to notify all the
inhabitants of the Town of Templeton, qualified to vote in
Elections and Town Affairs, to meet in the Narragansett
Regional High School Auditorium in said Templeton on
Saturday, March 7, next, at 1:30 P. M. then and there to act on
the following articles.[33]

Towns by by-law may designate the hour at which the annual meeting shall commence, the hours during which the polls may be open, and with the exceptions of the election of officers and matters required by law to be determined by ballot stipulate the hour after which all business shall be considered or that all business shall be considered by adjournment to another day.[34] A town may schedule the election of town officers to be held within seven days before or after the annual meeting at which business is transacted provided the time and place(s) for the election are stated in the warrant for the annual meeting; the election is deemed to be part of the annual town meeting.[35] In the larger towns it is common practice to hold town elections on one day and consider all business at an adjourned session on another day. Agawam and Saugus are unusual in that town officials are elected in November.

Several different methods are utilized by the various towns to nominate candidates for town offices. In all towns candidates for town offices can have their names placed upon the ballot by filing with the town clerk nomination papers signed by registered voters equal in number to one per cent of the vote cast for Governor in the town in the previous state election but no fewer than twenty nor more than fifty voters.[36] In a number of towns it is assumed incumbents are running for re-election unless the town clerk receives a written communication to the contrary.

In towns with non-partisan elections nominations may be made by one of two caucus systems authorized by the general laws.[37] Each caucus system is basically the same. The caucus is called by the selectmen and is called to order by the town clerk until a chairman is

---

[33] Templeton, Massachusetts, *Annual Reports of the Town Officers and Committees of the Town of Templeton, Massachusetts for the year ending December 31, 1963*, pp. 166-67.

[34] *Massachusetts General Laws*, chap. 39, sec. 22.

[35] *Ibid.*, chap. 39, sec. 23.

[36] *Ibid.*, chap. 53, sec. 6.

[37] *Ibid.*, chap. 53, sec. 117 and 121.

elected. The town clerk may not be elected clerk of the caucus or any other caucus officer. The chairman of the caucus is elected for only that caucus, but often is elected chairman of caucuses held in subsequent years. His duties are somewhat comparable to those of the moderator at town meetings. The town meeting "may determine whether nominations shall be made separately or partly or wholly on one ballot, and may within the limits defined by law, prescribe the day and hour when such caucus shall be held and how long the polls shall be kept open, and make provision for the preparation and use of ballots."[38] In Wellesley, for example, an adjourned session of the annual town meeting on April 29, 1940 voted that caucuses shall be held at least twenty-five days prior to the town election commencing at 8 p.m. and the polls shall be kept open until 10 p.m. or later if the caucus so determines. One ballot prepared by the town clerk is given to each voter as he enters the hall.[39] Candidates nominated by caucus are so designated on the ballot and may benefit from this designation. Holden did away with the caucus because most candidates defeated in the caucus filed nomination petitions and ran in the town elections.

Towns which have partisan elections hold caucuses under provisions of the general laws.[40] Candidates may run in the caucus of each party. In Webster in 1961, for example, four Democrats entered both the Democratic and Republican caucuses; two Democrats were nominated by the Democratic caucus and two were nominated by the Republican caucus.[41]

The arrangement of the names of candidates for town offices on the ballot is governed by general law. Candidates for re-election are listed first on the election ballot in alphabetical order by office followed by non-incumbents listed in alphabetical order by office.[42]

Towns which have been divided into voting precincts may allow precinct voting for the election of town officers at the annual meeting and at special elections. The town clerk and the board of registrars are required to canvass the returns from the several precincts and declare immediately the results.[43] Absentee voting is allowed in ninety-

---

[38] *Ibid.*, chap 53, sec. 121.

[39] Letter from Mrs. Mary C. Ditano, Town Clerk of Wellesley, Massachusetts, August 14, 1964.

[40] *Massachusetts General Laws,* chap. 53, sec. 71-116.

[41] Howard S. Knowles, "How Massachusetts Towns Choose Their Officers," *Sunday Telegram* (Worcester, Massachusetts), February 12, 1961, p. B-1

[42] *Massachusetts General Laws,* chap. 54, sec. 42.

[43] *Ibid.*, chap. 39, sec. 21.

nine towns which have accepted an enabling statute providing for absentee voting at regular town elections.[44]

Elections in most towns are non-partisan. Twenty-five towns with open town meetings hold partisan elections: Belchertown, Canton, Clinton, Douglas, Dudley, East Longmeadow, Granby, Great Barrington, Hampden, Lee, Lenox, Maynard, Monson, Northfield, Palmer, Russell, Sandisfield, Seekonk, Sheffield, Southbridge, Southwick, Ware, Webster, West Stockbridge, and Wilbraham. Six towns with representative town meetings hold partisan elections: Agawam, Easthampton, Framingham, Greenfield, Montague, and West Springfield. There has been talk in a few towns with non-partisan elections of adopting partisan elections, but no town has done so.

State officials of the two parties generally look favorably upon partisan elections as one means of strengthening the party by keeping the party organization intact and functioning in the off state election years. The opinion is expressed by a few that under a system of partisan elections patronage can be utilized to recruit persons to serve on party committees. Occasionally it is maintained that partisan elections would increase citizen interest in town government, but an examination of the per cent of registered voters who voted in the 1964 partisan and non-partisan town elections does not clearly bear out this contention. Forty-two to seventy-five per cent of the eligible voters in towns with partisan elections voted in the 1964 election; an average of approximately two-thirds of the eligible voters. Although the average voter turnout in towns with non-partisan elections was somewhat less than in towns with partisan elections in 1964, many towns with non-partisan elections had a voter turnout exceeding seventy-five per cent. Edgartown had a ninety-one per cent turnout, Petersham and Upton had a ninety per cent turnout, and Millville and Tyngsborough had an eighty-eight per cent turnout of eligible voters.

It is logical to anticipate that voter turnout would be higher in towns with partisan elections as it is in the personal interest of each party committee to secure the largest possible turnout of voters favorable to the party. The Framingham Democratic town committee in 1966 conducted a "voter incentive" project: A drawing was held to award a fifty dollar cash prize to a Democratic or independent voter who cast his ballot in the town elections. In consequence, in partisan towns you have apathetic and disinterested citizens voting who have

---

[44] *Ibid.*, chap. 54, sec. 103A.

been brought to the polls or pressured into going to the polls by the party. Whether the ends of democracy are better served by pressuring voters to the polls is debatable.

The Massachusetts Selectman editorialized in 1953 that towns with partisan elections should "re-examine the situation to see if it would not be desirable to turn to a non-partisan system."[45] The old cliche that "there is no Democratic or Republican way to pave streets or collect rubbish" is a truism. Partisan politics contribute nothing of positive value to but do complicate town administration.

A bill filed in the 1964 General Court provided for the abolition of partisan elections in Canton subject to a town referendum but was referred to the next annual session, a method used to kill bills without voting to defeat them.[46] However, the General Court allowed Watertown to hold a referendum; partisan elections were abandoned on March 7, 1966 by a vote of 5,242 to 3,520.[47]

The Democratic and Republican town committees in towns with partisan elections usually play an active role in the recruitment of candidates and the election campaign. In Maynard, however, the town committees are not active and in Sandisfield are active occasionally.

In most towns with non-partisan elections the Democratic and Republican town committees play no active role in town elections. Exceptions include Avon, Boylston, Hudson, Mansfield, Norwell, Oxford, Pepperell, Rockland, Sharon, Shutesbury, Stockbridge, Sturbridge, West Bridgewater, and Winchendon. In these towns it is not unusual to discover that only one town committee is active: the Republican town committee, for example, in Boylston.

Citizen associations which recruit or endorse candidates for town officers are found in a few towns. Frequently, these associations prove to be temporary and die a natural death following one or two elections. Needham had a citizen association which played a somewhat unsuccessful role in one election and expired. In Cummington an adult discussion group until 1962 usually recruited candidates to run for town offices, but at present a majority of the members of the group hold elective town office. Millville has a Good Government Association and a Progressive Party. In Medway caucuses are held by the Good Government Association, the Progressive Association, and the

---

[45] *The Massachusetts Selectman,* September 1953, p. 5.

[46] *Massachusetts General Court,* House No. 1679, 1964.

[47] Letter from George B. Wellman, Town Clerk, Watertown, Massachusetts, March 28, 1966.

25

Republicans. In a few towns with non-partisan elections the citizen associations represent the Democratic and Republican parties under different names. A citizen association may gain dominance in town elections. To cite only one example, the 1965 and 1966 slates of candidates selected by the Paxton Citizens Town Committee were unchallenged.

"Know Your Candidates Night" is sponsored by civic associations in many towns; these meetings most commonly are sponsored by the League of Women Voters. However, the sponsor is the Chamber of Commerce in Auburn, the Parent-Teacher Association in Grafton, the Junior Chamber of Commerce in Shrewsbury, and the Junior Chamber of Commerce and Woman's Club in Oxford. At these meetings candidates for town offices are introduced, permitted to speak briefly, and answer questions raised by the audience.

In 1964, of 158 towns surveyed there were no contests for town offices in fourteen towns, there was one more candidate than there were offices to be filled in twelve towns, and there were two more candidates than there were offices to be filled in ten towns. In general, the smaller towns have the fewest contests for office although the largest town, Brookline, had a contest for only one office in 1966. In recent years the sharp rise in school expenditures and the concern over the quality of the schools have resulted in increased competition for seats on the school committee. Personalities often appear to be more important than issues in determining the winners in contests for town offices.

The town of Saugus had a unique election system in that the five member board of selectmen and the five member school committee were elected by proportional representation in 1948 and 1950.[48] Proportional representation was repealed by the voters on February 26, 1951 when they accepted a statute providing for the substitution of plurality voting.[49]

Brookline has been using mechanical voting machines in town elections since 1941 and its lead has been followed by Concord, East Longmeadow, Greenfield, Lee, Lexington, Northbridge, Otis, Sudbury, Swampscott, and West Springfield. Winthrop abandoned the use of machines in 1965 because older citizens complained referenda questions were difficult to read. Amesbury, Lenox, Newburyport, and

---

[48] *Massachusetts Acts of 1947*, chap. 17, sec. 2 and 4.
[49] *Massachusetts Acts of 1951*, chap. 79.

Winchester used voting machines for the first time in the September 10, 1964 primary election.[50] Voting machines are more accurate and faster than hand counting of ballots and over a period of ten or more years are cheaper than hand counting. The initial cost of the mechanical machines and the space required for storage between elections are responsible for the small number of towns using machines. The development of less expensive electronic ballott counting machines promises to revolutionize the counting of ballotts in Massachusetts towns.

In 1966, Braintree experimented with the I.B.M. votomatic system; voters were provided with punch-card ballots listing candidates for ninety-six offices. Upon the close of the polls, the ballots were transported to a central computer loaned by a local business firm. Election results were available in three hours and thirty-one minutes compared to an average of twelve and one-half hours required to count ballots by hand in previous elections. The town clerk reported that the counting of ballots would have been completed in a shorter period of time if forty-four ballots had not been damaged and required re-punching.

The votomatic balloting system is fast and produces an accurate count by eliminating human counting errors; voters expressed their approval. However, the system suffers from one disadvantage. Votomatic election ballots do not permit the listing of all candidates in a preliminary election on one page; candidates listed on page two and subsequent pages would be at a disadvantage. Furthermore, the votomatic system does not eliminate the hand counting of write-in votes and absentee ballots.

The Recall

The special acts creating a town manager plan of administration in Arlington, Mansfield, Middleborough, Norwood, Provincetown, Saugus, and Stoughton provide for the recall of elected officials. In Stoughton, for example, any registered voter is authorized "to file with the town clerk an affidavit containing the name of the officer sought to be recalled and a statement of the grounds of recall."[51] The town clerk must supply the filer of the affidavit with recall petitions which must be signed by two hundred registered voters and returned to the town clerk within twenty days. Upon the certification of the

---

[50] *The Boston Globe,* September 7, 1964, p. 21.
[51] *Massachusetts Acts of 1921,* chap. 400, sec. 21-27.

petition signatures by the registrars of voters, the town clerk immediately transmits the petition to the selectmen who forthwith must notify the town official mentioned in the recall petition. If the town official fails to resign within five days, the selectmen must call a special election to be held on a Tuesday within twenty-five days "of the date of the town clerk's certificate that a sufficient petition is filed." If a town election is scheduled to be held within sixty days of the date on the town clerk's certificate, the selectmen may hold the recall election in conjunction with the scheduled election.

Any town official who is the object of a recall petition may be a candidate to succeed himself. A town official may not be recalled during his first three months in office and any other town official who was not recalled in a recall election may not be recalled for at least three months after the first recall election.

The recall seldom has been used in Massachusetts. Three of the five Norwood selectmen voted to fire the town manager in 1939; this action led to a successful campaign to recall these three selectmen and replace them with individuals favorable to the manager. The citizens believed the charges against the manager were nebulous. He was cleared of the charges and reinstated following the recall of the three anti-manager selectmen.[52] Saugus voters recalled three of the five selectmen in 1961 because the three selectmen had licensed a liquor store near a boy scout camp.[53]

Conduct of Business

All mundane matters, major or trivial, affecting the town may be brought before the town meeting to be debated and decided. Each article in the warrant is taken up and considered; the consideration may be no more than a motion and a vote "to pass over" the article.

At the typical town meeting debate tends to be practical rather than philosophical in nature. Its quality varies from the dull, shallow, specious, and the superfluous to the didactic and the profound. A certain amount of levity often is interjected in the debates. Usually at least on voter will refer to what the tax rate was in 1933 or some other year and condemn excessive spending. On a zoning issue a voter may say "you buy a piece of property and you cannot do what

---

[52] Donald B. Leiffer, "Town Manager in Massachusetts" (Unpublished Ph.D. dissertation, Harvard University, 1939), pp. 262-78.
[53] *Worcester Telegram* (Massachusetts), August 24, 1961, p. 6.

28

you want with it" and a second voter may accuse the planning board of "representing the people across the street instead of the whole town." However, debate in general is sensible. Unfortunately, the use of humor or an appeal to prejudice may prove more effective than the use of reason.

Viva Voce voting most commonly is used, but show of hands, standing votes, division of the meeting, a roll call, and written ballots may be used. A roll call seldom is demanded because it is too time consuming in most towns. Secret ballots are used in voting on highly emotional issues to protect voters who fear recriminations if their votes were public. Secret ballot voting is slow and depending upon the number of ballots cast may take thirty or more minutes to cast the ballots and another fifteen or more minutes to count the ballots.

Articles are voted authorizing the town treasurer with the approval of the selectmen to borrow funds in anticipation of tax revenue, the purchase of land, the selectmen to employ counsel and defend the town against any suit brought against it, the creation of an unpaid committee to study the advisability of establishing a regional vocational school district, and the transfer of a street light from one pole to a second pole on the same street. Other articles are voted accepting the reports of committees and a street for plowing, fixing the salary and compensation of elective town officers, appropriating funds for vocational education and land damages resulting from street improvements, instructing the assessors to use a specified sum from free cash to reduce the tax rate, and changing the zone of a strip of land from commercial to residential. The town budget usually is the most important article adopted at the town meeting and varies from several thousand dollars in the smallest towns to $18,088,436.49 in Brookline in 1963.[54]

Certain actions of the open town meeting in Marblehead have been subject to referendum since 1954. Any vote appropriating "fifty thousand dollars or more as a special appropriation or establishing a new board or office or abolishing an old board or office or merging two or more boards or offices, or fixing the term of office of town officers, where such term is optional, or increasing or reducing the number of members of a board, or adopting a new by-law, or amending an existing by-law, shall not be operative until the expiration of five days, exclusive of Sundays and holidays, from the dissolution of

---

[54] Brookline, Massachusetts, *Brookline Town Report,* 1963, p. 292.

the meeting, nor, if a petition for referendum thereon has been filed, until the question of ratification of such vote has been determined in the manner herein provided."[55] A referendum must be held if petitions are signed by three hundred registered voters and the town meeting actions submitted to the voters for determination are reversed by majority vote provided at least twenty per cent of the registered voters so vote. In 1956, the voters in a referendum reversed by a vote of 3873 to 2141 the approval by the town meeting of an article providing for the revaluation of property; a referendum on the same subject was held on March 21, 1966.[56] Prior to the adoption of a representative town meeting in 1948, Norwood voters were authorized by a 1939 special act to use the referendum.[57]

A presiding officer and procedural rules are essential at town meetings to protect the rights of individuals and minorities and also to facilitate the efficient conduct of business. Procedural rules for town meetings are contained in the general laws of the Commonwealth and in many town by-laws. A town is authorized by general law to adopt by-laws for the regulation of the town meeting.[58]

Mr. Moderator. The earliest town meetings were small and apparently did not have moderators as the town records contain no references to them. The first order of business at an early town meeting was the election of a moderator for the meeting. The General Court in 1715 required each town to elect a moderator who was empowered to manage and regulate the meeting and no one was permitted to speak without permission from the moderator.[59]

The moderator is the cynosure of the town meeting as he is its presiding officer. He is a gentleman of great respect, parliamentary skill, and tact. Occasionally a woman is elected moderator.[60] The moderator is not required to be a registered voter of the town as the laws of the Commonwealth are silent on this point, but in practice always is a registered voter.

The moderator may be elected for each meeting as the first order of business at the meeting or for a term of one or three years by

---

[55] *Massachusetts Acts of 1954,* chap. 405.
[56] *The Boston Sunday Herald,* February 6, 1966, p. 11.
[57] *Massachusetts Acts of 1939,* chap. 79.
[58] *Massachusetts General Laws,* chap. 39, sec. 15.
[59] *The Acts and Resolves of the Province of the Massachusetts Bay,* Vol. II (Boston: Wright and Potter, 1874), p. 30.
[60] The moderator in Billerica in 1966 was a woman.

ballot with the use of the voting list at the meeting for the election of town officers.[61] In only a few towns is he elected for each meeting. Most moderators are elected to one year terms with re-election to another one year term nearly automatic. Prior to assuming office the moderator is sworn "to the faithful performance of his duties" by the town clerk.[62]

If the office of moderator becomes vacant for any reason, the town elects a new moderator. In the absence of the moderator a temporary moderator must be elected. Until a moderator is elected the town clerk presides at the meeting but if he is absent, the chairman of the selectmen presides or in his absence, the senior selectman.[63]

The moderator's duties are spelled out by statute and supplemented by by-laws and customs in many towns. Consequently, the practices of the moderator vary from town to town. Each town has its own personality which is reflected in the manner in which the town meeting is conducted; the moderator may follow the rule book closely or he may conduct the meeting on a relatively informal basis as long as the meeting runs smoothly. If a motion is made which is not on the warrant, the moderator cannot accept it as an official motion, but may accept it as an unofficial motion to take the sense of the meeting provided no voter objects to the procedure.

A town meeting may be held in more than one building provided the buildings have been equipped with a common public address system which enables all registered voters in each building to hear and participate in the proceedings.[64] The moderator may appoint an assistant moderator to preside in each of the other buildings who possesses all the powers of the moderator with one exception: He may not recognize a citizen seeking the floor without first obtaining permission from the moderator.[65] The use of more than two buildings is unusual. However, four separate halls were used by the 1965 Marblehead annual town meeting because the warrant contained several highly controversial articles.

If the moderator determines that there are inadequate places for all voters who wish to participate in the town meeting or voters in attendance are not being afforded an opportunity to participate for any reason, he may recess the meeting until later in the day or upon

---

[61] *Massachusetts General Laws,* chap. 39, sec. 14.
[62] *Ibid.,* chap. 41, sec. 107.
[63] *Ibid.,* chap. 39, sec. 14.
[64] *Ibid.,* chap 39, sec. 10.
[65] *Ibid.,* chap. 39, sec. 14.

consultation with the selectmen present adjourn the meeting for up to fourteen days when facilities to accommodate all voters who wish to attend and participate can be made available.[66]

At the time specified in the warrant for the start of the meeting the moderator raps his gavel and states "the meeting will come to order." The moderator in some towns, most commonly ones with many new voters, explains at the beginning of the meeting the basic procedural rules; this is a sound practice which facilitates the smooth conduct of the meeting. Should the town clerk be absent or the office vacant, the first business conducted is the election by ballot of a temporary town clerk.[67] The clerk reads the warrant and the return of the service thereof unless it is moved and carried that the reading be dispensed with. The moderator commonly requests unanimous consent to refer to articles by subject matter instead of reading them in their entirety. Articles are considered in the order in which they appear in the warrant unless the meeting votes to consider articles out of order. In Wayland, for example, an article may be considered out of order by a two-thirds vote of the meeting.[68]

The moderator as presiding officer of the town meeting is in charge of the proceedings, decides all points of law, publicly declares all votes, and in open meeting may administer the oath of office to any town officer elected thereat.[69] If seven or more registered voters immediately challenge a vote declared by the moderator, he verifies it either by dividing or polling the voters unless the by-laws provide for a different method of verification.[70] The moderator must accept the vote of any individual whose name appears on the voting list or who presents a certificate issued by the registrars of voters certifying he is a registered voter.[71]

No one may address a town meeting without the permission of the moderator and at his request every person must be silent. An individual who continues to act in a disorderly manner after a warning from the moderator may be ordered to leave the meeting and may

---

[66] *Ibid.*, chap. 39, sec. 10.

[67] *Ibid.*, chap. 41, sec. 14.

[68] Wayland, Massachusetts, *By-Laws of the Town of Wayland, Massachusetts*, art. 2, sec. 3.

[69] *Massachusetts General Laws*, chap. 39, sec. 15.

[70] *Ibid.*

[71] *Ibid.*, chap. 39, sec. 18.

be ejected from the meeting and confined by a constable until the meeting has adjourned.[72]

A moderator may address the town meeting during the course of debate, but it is preferable for the moderator to enter the debate only if he steps down as presiding officer and allows a temporary moderator to preside. A moderator may vote in any open town meeting provided he is a registered voter of the town, but his vote is not needed except to break a tie or defeat a motion by creating a tie. In general, moderators do not exercise their right to vote.

Aside from conducting the meeting one of the duties commonly assigned to the moderator by the town meeting is the appointment of various committees. In Walpole, for example, the moderator appoints the Appropriation Committee, Personnel Board, Permanent Advisory Building Committee, Committee to Study Future School Needs, Old Post Road School Building Committee, East Street School Building Committee, Committee on Boyden School Addition, Committee on Taking Over Rural and Maple Grove Cemeteries, Committee on Land for Future Schools, Committee to Review Town Charter and By-laws, Water Committee, Committee on Street Names, Committee on Maintenance of Town Parks and Playgrounds, Vocational School Study Committee, and Committee for Plans and Specifications for a New Junior High School.[73] In certain towns, the town meeting votes to authorize the moderator and selectmen jointly to appoint study committees.

Statutory provisions dealing with the moderator's powers and duties commonly are supplemented by town by-laws. In Oxford the moderator may require that all motions submitted for consideration be in writing; citizens must stand while speaking and address the moderator; motions to lay on the table, to take from the table, or to change the order of business are non-debatable; no action may be taken on the report of a committee appointed at a previous town meeting unless the report is noted in the warrant calling the meeting; and *Cushing's Manual of Parliamentary Practice* must be used to settle disputes involving parliamentary procedure.[74]

The Kingston by-laws stipulate that all motions involving the expenditure of funds must be submitted in writing and the moderator

---

[72] *Ibid.*, chap. 39, sec. 17.

[73] Walpole, Massachusetts, *Annual Report* 1963, pp. 6-7.

[74] Oxford, Massachusetts, *By-Laws of the Town of Oxford, Massachusetts,* art. 2, sec. 3-6.

33

may direct other motions to be submitted in writing; speakers recognized by the moderator must confine their remarks to the question under consideration and must avoid personalities; all committees shall be appointed by the moderator unless the meeting otherwise directs; *Robert's Rules of Order* is to be used to settle parliamentary questions where applicable to the town meeting; and the moderator "may speak to points of order in preference to all other persons." [75]

The Berlin by-laws stipulate non-voters may not be admitted to the floor of the hall except newspaper reporters and guests at the discretion of the moderator; the moderator determines the boundaries of the floor of the hall, may entertain a motion to consider an article out of order, and may refuse to entertain frivolous motions; a motion may not be made to dissolve a meeting until every article has been acted upon; the order of precedence of various motions and the method of taking votes is specified; no person may speak more than twice on a question except to answer an inquiry without obtaining leave of the meeting; and all committees shall be appointed by the moderator unless the meeting otherwise directs.[76]

The Attorney General of the Commonwealth approved a by-law adopted by the 1963 Spencer annual town meeting which stipulates that a handbook prepared by a committee of the Massachusetts Moderators' Association shall be used to settle disputes involving parliamentary procedures.[77] The use of this handbook as a guide for town meeting procedures is preferable to the use of *Cushing's Manual of Parliamentary Practice* and *Robert's Rules of Order* which were not specifically designed to apply to town meetings. Furthermore, the Supreme Judicial Court has questioned the applicability of *Robert's Rules of Order* to town meetings.

> Coming directly to §68 of Robert's Rules of Order Revised, we are at once struck by its dubious application of town meeting government. The phrase "regular business meeting" would be an inept description of a town meeting, whether annual or special. The phrase "previous regular business meeting" would be even more inept. The two phrases in the same sentence must refer to the same type of meeting. Even by forced construction, the phrase "previous regular business meeting" would run counter to statute and to settled law.[78]

[75] Kingston, Massachusetts, *By-Laws, Rules and Regulations of the Town of Kingston, Massachusetts,* art. II, sec. 3, 4, 6, 9, and 10.

[76] Berlin, Massachusetts, *By-Laws of the Town of Berlin, Massachusetts,* art. II, sec. 4-10.

[77] Richard B. Johnson, Benjamin A. Trustman, and Charles Y. Wadsworth, *Town Meeting Time* (Boston: Little, Brown and Company, 1962).

[78] *Blomquist v. Town of Arlington,* 338 Mass. 598 (1959).

The Supreme Judicial Court has ruled that town meeting procedures generally conform to the customary rules of parliamentary procedure, yet a town meeting is not required to conform to the strict rules of parliamentary procedure.[79] Although the rules of parliamentary procedure for legislative bodies require the same vote for the adoption of a motion to rescind as the original measure required, the rules do not apply to a town meeting.[80] At an adjourned session of a town meeting, a reconsideration of a vote taken in the first session of the meeting revokes the vote and it ceases to have any effect.[81]

Role of the Town Clerk. The town clerk normally is the second most important individual at the town meeting and sits at a table near the moderator on the stage or at the head of the hall. He records the transactions of the town meeting as declared by the moderator and is required to count and enter in the records the votes on articles which by statute require a two-thirds vote for passage.[82] The clerk records all unanimous votes on such articles in the records as unanimous and a count is not taken. A town clerk may correct a mistake in his records, but the Supreme Judicial Court has ruled that the town clerk's records are the official records of the proceedings of the town meeting and may not be changed nor oral evidence utilized to correct omissions.[83]

Town by-laws often spell out the duties of the town clerk with respect to the town meeting. For instance, the Leicester clerk following a vote to adjourn a meeting to another day must post in a public place in each precinct and on his bulletin board in the entry of the town hall "a statement of the day and hour to which the adjournment voted and of the business remaining to come before the meeting." [84] In addition, he must notify in writing all committee members appointed or elected at the meeting "stating the business upon which they are to act and the names of the persons composing the committee, and also to notify all officers, boards, and committees of all votes passed . . . in any way affecting them; and further after each Annual Meeting to post and maintain on the bulletin board

---

[79] *Wood v. Town of Milton*, 197 Mass. 531 (1908).
[80] *Adams v. Cook*, 245 Mass. 543 (1923).
[81] *Withington v. Inhabitants of the Town of Harvard*, 62 Mass. 66 (1851).
[82] *Massachusetts General Laws*, chap. 39, sec. 15.
[83] *Taylor v. Henry*, 19 Mass. 397 (1824).
[84] Leicester, Massachusetts, *Revised By-Laws of the Town of Leicester, Massachusetts*, chap 2, sec. 6.

in the Town Hall a corrected list of all elected and appointed officers of the Town." [85]

Role of the Town Counsel. The town counsel, an attorney specializing in municipal law, customarily is present at all town meetings in most towns to provide the meetings with legal advice in response to frequent questions from the floor directed to him through the moderator. In many towns he prepares for the selectmen most of the articles which are inserted in the warrant and many of the motions, affirmative and negative, to be made at the town meeting. Henry W. Hardy has written:

> Many a town meeting bogs down when a point of order is raised that a motion is "not within the scope of the article." It behooves the town counsel, therefore, so to phrase the articles as to permit a reasonable latitude for town meeting action. He should take particular care in drafting articles relating to by-laws, borrowing, and land acquisition, for votes under these articles are bound to come under close scrutiny later by, among others, the attorney general, counsel for lending banks and conveyancers.[86]

Many legal problems arise at town meetings; articles inserted by petition of voters may be legally defective and the moderator in many towns confers with the counsel on complex legal questions and he may be asked to give his legal opinion on an article prior to a vote being taken. On exceptionally complex legal questions the moderator may declare a recess to confer privately with the counsel.

Three experts on town meetings warn the moderator that the town counsel usually prepares articles inserted in the warrant by the selectmen at the request of boards and officers and the motions to be made after conferring with the Attorney General or a bond counsel and, consequently, the moderator should be wary of publicly disagreeing with motions prepared by the counsel. If the moderator "is troubled by a motion prepared by town counsel he would do well to declare a recess and consult him privately. The face he saves may be his own."[87]

The dissolution of the meeting does not end the town counsel's work in connection with the meeting. If the meeting has so voted, he must examine titles to property, initiate eminent domain proceedings, draw up deeds, prepare petitions for submission to the General Court,

---

[85] *Ibid.,* chap. 3, sec. 2.
[86] Henry W. Hardy, *The Role of the Town Counsel* (Amherst: Bureau of Government Research, University of Massachusetts, 1960), p. 11.
[87] Johnson, Trustman, and Wadsworth, *Town Meeting Time,* p. 30.

36

prepare contracts, and meet with state officials and town committees.[88] The increasing volume of legal affairs prompted the 1965 Framingham annual town meeting to appropriate funds for a full time town counsel.

Role of the Finance Committee. The finance committee performs a watchdog advisory function for the town meeting. Any town may provide for the appointment or election of an advisory, appropriations, or finance committee and all towns with valuations exceeding one million dollars for the purpose of apportioning the state tax must provide for the appointment or election of such a committee.[89] The finance committee by by-law may continue in office for a maximum term of three years with the duties of studying any or all town questions, reporting on same, and submitting at the annual town meeting a budget unless a by-law charges the selectmen with the duty of its submission. [90] Approximately one-fourth of the finance committees limit their study and report to articles appropriating money; the committees in other towns study and report on all articles.

The finance committee's recommendations distributed to the voters prior to the town meeting are advisory only and not binding in any manner. Commonly its recommendation on an article is offered as a motion by a member of the committee. The Supreme Judicial Court has ruled that the failure of the finance committee to hold a public hearing as authorized by town by-law on the question of raising funds for a proposed building did not invalidate the vote on the article in the warrant on the question.[91]

Other Town Meeting Officials. The warrant for a town meeting prepared by the selectmen is directed to the constables of the town or other specified persons "who give notice of such meeting in the manner prescribed by the by-laws, or, if there are no by-laws, by a vote of the town, or in a manner approved by the attorney general."[92] In Athol, for example, the constable who serves the warrant for a town meeting is required at the same time to mail an attested copy of the warrant to each member of the finance committee.[93] The constable

---

[88] Hardy, *Town Counsel,* p. 10.
[89] *Massachusetts General Laws,* chap. 39, sec. 16.
[90] *Ibid.*
[91] *Young v. Town of Westport,* 302 Mass. 597 (1939).
[92] *Massachusetts General Laws,* chap. 39, sec. 10.
[93] Athol, Massachusetts, *By-Laws of the Town of Athol, Massachusetts,* chap. III, sec. 2.

also acts as a sergeant-at-arms at the town meeting; the moderator is authorized to direct a constable to remove a disorderly person from a town meeting and confine him until the meeting is adjourned.[94]

The board of selectmen or the town clerk appoints checkers whose duty is to ensure that only registered voters are allowed to enter the town meeting floor. When a vote on an article must be counted the moderator of the larger town meetings appoints tellers to help him take the count; the tellers in a number of towns are sworn to faithfully perform their duties. The moderator may appoint tellers either prior to or during a meeting and obviously should not appoint as a teller a voter who has a personal interest in or wishes to participate in the debate on a highly controversial and important issue.

In towns which have adopted precinct voting a warden under the supervision of the town clerk is in charge of each voting precinct. Larger town meetings utilize high school students as page boys to deliver messages, run errands, set up chairs, and pass the portable microphone to citizens recognized as speakers by the moderator.

Quorum Requirement. The general laws of the Commonwealth do not establish nor do they require towns to establish a quorum for town meetings. A quorum is the minimum number of registered voters specified by the by-laws of the town who must be present at a town meeting for legal action to be taken on the articles included in the warrant. A number of voters less than a quorum is authorized to adjourn a town meeting and this is the only legal action that can be taken.[95]

Surprisingly, a number of towns have failed to establish a quorum requirement and many towns have established a quorum requirement so low as to be meaningless as a means of offering protection to the town by guaranteeing adequate *de facto* representation to voters not in attendance. To ensure representation for every section of a large town at an open town meeting, a quorum requirement could be established stipulating the minimum number of voters from each precinct or section of the town who must be present before the town meeting legally can conduct business; such a requirement would make it difficult for a section of a town to pack a meeting to ensure passage of a favorable article.

---

[94] *Massachusetts General Laws,* chap. 39, sec. 17.
[95] *Ibid.,* chap. 39, sec. 13.

A survey of 158 towns in 1964 revealed that 36 towns have no quorum requirement for the annual town meeting. Most of these towns have a relatively small population. However, included in the list are Acton (10,188), Barnstable (15,609), Concord (14,516), Grafton (11,571), Lynnfield (9,821), Orange (6,206), Sharon (11,341), Spencer (8,514), Wakefield (25,571), Westport (8,200), and Williamstown (7,042).

Citizens opposed to the establishment of a quorum requirement maintain that the lack of a quorum requirement stimulates citizens to attend town meetings in order to protect their rights. A survey of attendance at the 1964 annual town meeting in towns which lack a quorum requirement does not bear out this contention as the attendance varied from eight to fifty-five per cent and averaged between twenty-five and thirty per cent of the registered voters. Those in favor of a quorum requirement contend it is absolutely essential to have one in a growing town to prevent policy determination by a minuscule number of voters.

The quorum requirement is only six in Mount Washington (53); seven in Heath (300), Huntington (1,454), Sheffield (2,355), and Shelburne (1,819); nine in Shutesbury (333); and ten in Chester (1,143), North Brookfield (3,608), Oakham (632), and West Brookfield (2,233). In a large number of towns the quorum requirement is less than fifty. Several towns have established the quorum requirement in terms of a percentage of the registered voters; two per cent in Dudley; four per cent in Hinsdale and Westborough; and ten per cent in Petersham, Plainfield, and Rawley. The town clerk of a community with a population slightly less than one thousand which has no quorum requirement reports "we insist on at least twenty-five" being present at town meetings.

The moderator should determine whether a quorum is present prior to calling the town meeting to order, and state the presence of a quorum in calling the meeting to order. A voter at any time has the right to challenge the presence of a quorum. If a quorum call is demanded after action has been taken on a particular article and less than a quorum is present, the action taken on the article remains in force and the only action that can be taken is to adjourn the meeting until a later date.

The quorum requirement for special town meetings is less than for the annual meeting in a few towns. For example, the quorum requirement for the annual town meeting is one hundred in Boylston and one hundred and seventy-five in Seekonk, whereas it is twenty-five in Boylston and one hundred in Seekonk for special town meetings. Millis is an exception in that it has no quorum requirement for its annual town meeting, but has a quorum requirement of ten per cent of the registered voters for special town meetings.

The fact quorum requirements are set low does not prevent quorum problems. Forty-five of the 158 towns surveyed in 1964 reported experiencing quorum problems, especially at special town meetings. It is not unusual for special town meetings to be adjourned for the lack of a quorum. The town clerk and other town officials occasionally have to "beat the bush" to round up the necessary number of voters. At least one town attempts to solve the problem by purposely starting the meeting late. Day sessions of the annual town meeting generally are sparsely attended as workingmen are not free to attend until evening. New Ashford at one time held afternoon and evening sessions of the annual town meeting, but dropped the afternoon session because of poor attendance.

Northborough selectmen in 1964 refused to insert an article in the warrant for a forthcoming town meeting to increase the quorum requirement from fifty voters to ten per cent of the registered voters because of the difficulty of attracting fifty voters to a special town meeting which was delayed one-half hour while fire department members were called to meet the quorum requirement.

In general, the absence of a quorum requirement at the annual meeting should cause no problem. However, a reasonable quorum requirement at a special town meeting would appear to be desirable to protect citizens from the possible danger of selfish pressure groups petitioning for and packing a special town meeting.

Role of Select Committees. Town meeting government traditionally has been citizen government and still relies heavily upon citizen committees of the town meeting elected by the voters or appointed by the moderator or the selectmen.

A select committee may be created by the passage of an article calling for the creation of the committee or as a result of a subsidiary motion to refer a subject being debated to a study committee. By-law revision, re-valuation, school construction, aerial ladder truck, representative town meeting, sewerage disposal plant, library, clerical help, town administration, a public works department, and regional planning are examples of subjects studied by select committees.

Although the moderator customarily is authorized to appoint committee members, "it is not clear whether a town moderator has the power to appoint a chairman. Many do, and in any event the moderator may charge one of the members with the duty of bringing the committee together and organizing it. This may amount to a tactful way of designating the chairman without causing the members of the committee to feel that they have been deprived of the opportunity of choosing their own chairman. No doubt the vote instructing the moderator to appoint the committee could instruct him to appoint the chairman, but in practice it seldom does." [96] The moderator's role with respect to a committee ends upon the appointment of its members; he possesses no supervisory powers over the committee but does fill vacancies as they occur.

Committee procedures usually are informal depending primarily upon the chairman. The number of meetings held by select committees and the amount of work conducted by committees varies considerably. There are committees which are hard working and devote untold hours to the study of the subject assigned, but other committees do relatively little work.

Role of Pressure Groups. Organized economic pressure groups play a legitimate role in bringing their views before the town meeting, yet such groups are relatively uncommon in Massachusetts towns. A survey of 158 towns in 1964 revealed that organized economic pressure groups were nonexistent or played a minor role in most towns. This finding is not particularly surprising in view of the relatively small size of most towns; economic stakes are not as great as in large cities.

Local taxpayers associations are the most common type of economic pressure group in towns, but have been declining in number and the existing ones are not very active. They seek to improve the efficiency of town government and keep taxes as low as possible. Examples of their activities include mailing a form letter to each voter prior to the town meeting in Orleans and representatives of the association attending finance committee meetings in Wayland. In general, these associations are inefficacious.

---

[96] Johnson, Trustman, and Wadsworth, *Town Meeting Time*, pp. 36-38.

Stories circulate relative to town employees packing town meetings to pressure adoption of articles beneficial to them. While town employees are among the most faithful attendees of town meetings, there is little evidence of them packing and controlling a meeting.

The League of Women Voters is the most common type of non-economic citizen group found in towns. In 1965, there were local leagues in fifty-nine towns, five area leagues comprising twelve towns, and provisional leagues in two towns. The League undertakes studies of town problems, issues public statements, and educates the citizenry by conducting public meetings including "Pre-town Meeting Meetings" and "Meet the Candidates Nights."

Other non-economic citizens groups are found in a few towns, but often fail to establish firm roots. In 1965, for example, the Westford Independent Citizens' Council was organized to promote efficient government and citizen participation in town affairs, and provide information to citizens.

Ad hoc citizen committees spring to life when highly controversial issues such as fluoridation of the water supply and certain urban renewal projects are raised in a town, but these committees are ephemeral in nature. In Stoneham, for example, the issue of an urban renewal project for the central square area found a committee for urban renewal, the Stoneham League of Women Voters, and the Stoneham Ministers' Association favoring the project which was opposed by an anti-redevelopment committee.[97] A Boxboro Businessmen's Association was formed in 1965 because businessmen believed that proposed zoning amendments would unduly restrict business firms.[98] Another example was the formation of the Ipswich Citizens Committee to oust the executive secretary plan from the town. In Wayland a "committee opposing overhead high tension lines" was organized to oppose a Boston Edison Company plan to run a high voltage transmission line through marsh land.[99]

Role of Factions. The relative absence of organized pressure groups in Massachusetts towns does not mean that conflict is absent. Factions or cliques with changing membership are found in most towns. The town meeting is the arbiter of any factional disputes that may exist. At one

[97] *The Boston Sunday Globe,* December 6, 1964, p. 59.
[98] *Ibid.,* April 18, 1965, p. 12.
[99] John A. Long, "N. E. Town Fights for Landscape," *The Christian Science Monitor,* February 13, 1965, p. 2.

time or other a split between a faction favoring conservatism and a faction favoring innovation is not unusual. In certain towns the factional split is socio-economic: The split is between the white collar and blue collar workers representing to a certain extent the "haves" and the "have nots." Rising income levels have tended to obliterate the sharp distinction between the "haves" and the "have nots," yet it still exists in a less noticeable form. The "haves" usually are more willing to spend town funds than the "have nots" for major town improvements such as new schools, a new fire station, or a new town hall.

Rapidly growing towns experience factionalism in the form of a division between the "natives" and the "newcomers" with the more parsimonious "natives" generally favoring the status quo and the "newcomers" demanding changes especially in the form of new and improved town services which push the town tax rate upward. To varying degrees in different towns, the "natives" tend to represent "blue collar" workers and the "newcomers" tend to be "white collar" workers. This cleavage is reflected in town organizations. Each faction tends to be most active in certain organizations within the town. "Newcomers" tend to be better educated than the "natives" and are active in organizations with an intellectual orientation such as the town historical society or library association. The headquarters for a clique of "natives" may be a local store or garage or other place where citizens congregate. The proprietor of such an establishment is apt to be one of the town's leading influentials and have a sizable personal following. In towns where the split is deep, the "natives" whose families have lived in the town for generations feel they have a proprietary interest in the town and regard it as their sacred duty to safeguard the town for posterity against the "newcomers" who are considered to be carpetbaggers or transients. The "natives" may fear that the transitory "newcomers" if elected to town office will initiate extravagant projects and leave the town prior to their completion or foist a diabolical scheme on the town; hence, it is preferable to have the "natives" run the town to prevent a town calamity. Unfortunately, if this view prevails and the "natives" completely dominate town elections and appointments, the town may suffer by its failure to take advantage of the services of talented "newcomers" as elected and appointed town officials. If the number of white collar "newcomers" is small, they pose no political threat to the "natives" and, consequently, the "newcomers" may find they are readily accepted and respected by the "natives."

Length of residence in a town usually influences a candidate's chance of winning a town election. "Newcomers" in many towns challenge the incumbent "natives" in town elections and more successfully as the influx of "newcomers" continues. However, "newcomers" often work outside the town during the day and are not able to establish as many close contacts with the citizens as the "natives." Further, the voters often prefer as town officials individuals employed in the town as they are more accessible than those employed outside the town.

In the smaller towns factionalism may reveal itself in the form of family connection with one family grouping pitted against another or against the rest of the town. In other towns the leadership of a prominent family may be accepted. Intermarriage between large established town families over a period of years substantially increases their political power if they choose to exercise it.

The open town meeting is not a perfect instrument for adjusting factional differences but functions as adequately as any substitute.

Non-Voters. Town by-laws usually stipulate that non-voters, "strangers," may be allowed to attend a town meeting with the approval of the moderator or the town meeting. The gallery or a section in the rear of the hall is set aside for non-voters who may not enter within the bounds of the town meeting floor. The Kingston by-laws, for example, stipulate the check list is to be "used in admitting voters to a town meeting, except that non-voters may be admitted to a defined and separate portion thereof, and non-voters may address the meeting if the meeting so voted."[100] Most by-laws are silent on the question whether non-voters may address the meeting.

Special Town Meetings

Selectmen may call a special town meeting at any time provided at least seven days notice is given and must include in the warrant all subjects requested in writing by one hundred registered voters or ten per cent of the registered voters whichever number is the lesser.[101]

Selectmen must call a special town meeting within forty-five days when requested to do so in writing by two hundred registered voters

---

[100] Kingston, Massachusetts, *By-Laws*, art. II, sec. 1.
[101] *Massachusetts General Laws*, chap. 39, sec. 9-10.

or twenty per cent of the registered voters whichever number is the lesser and insert in the warrant all articles requested in the petition.[102] If the selectmen unreasonably refuse to call a town meeting, a justice of the peace may issue a warrant for a town meeting if requested to call one in writing by one hundred registered voters or ten per cent of the registered voters.[103]

Any number of town meetings for distinct purposes may be called by the same warrant.[104] An important matter can be considered in the first meeting scheduled and other business may be taken up in the second meeting scheduled for later the same evening when attendance is apt to be less. And action taken at the first meeting cannot be reconsidered by the second meeting. However, it is more common for two separate warrants to be issued calling two distinct special meetings for the same evening. Northborough, for example, scheduled one meeting to begin at 7:30 p.m. and a second meeting to begin at 7:35 p.m. on June 22, 1964. The moderator called the first meeting to order at 7:30 p.m. and a motion was made and carried to recess the meeting to take up the articles on the warrant of the second town meeting scheduled for 7:35 p.m. The second meeting was called to order and after the conclusion of its business it was adjourned and the first meeting reconvened. The typical reason for two meetings on the same evening is a development requiring relatively prompt town meeting action which arose after the warrant for a special town meeting had been closed. A second warrant is issued calling a second town meeting for the same evening provided the required warning can be given; this was the reason why Northborough held two special town meetings the same evening.

Special town meetings are held in many towns during the last month or two of the calendar year for the purpose of transferring funds from certain accounts to depleted accounts. In other towns the need to hold special town meetings for this purpose has been obviated by establishing a reserve account and authorizing the finance committee in its discretion to transfer funds from the reserve account to depleted accounts; such a policy is a sound one as it provides the necessary fiscal flexibility by authorizing an informed citizen committee, which continually has been exercising oversight over town finance, to transfer funds and thereby avoid the expense of holding a special town meeting which few citizens would attend.

---

[102] *Ibid.*, chap. 39, sec. 10.
[103] *Ibid.*, chap. 39, sec. 12.
[104] *Ibid.*, chap. 39, sec. 10.

The small attendance at the average special town meeting argues against the calling of a special town meeting unless it is essential that one must be held or a large turnout of voters can be predicted. However, there is much merit in calling a special town meeting to consider an important and highly controversial issue that could be considered at the annual town meeting. The annual meeting warrant in most towns is of such length that an important and highly controversial issue may not receive adequate consideration or action may be postponed.

By-Laws

By-laws are town laws enacted by the town meeting and if not repugnant to law have the same validity as statutes enacted by the General Court.[105] Any by-law approved by a town meeting and proof of compliance with procedural requirements for the adoption of by-laws must be submitted by the town clerk to the Attorney General of the Commonwealth for his approval; a by-law so submitted becomes effective when approved by the Attorney General or after ninety days without action by the Attorney General.[106] The penalty for a breach of a by-law is determined by the town, but may not exceed fifty dollars for each offense.[107] The Supreme Judicial Court has ruled that every presumption is in favor of the validity of a by-law.[108] A "by-law is more than a mere rule of parliamentary procedure. It is a protective measure designed to safeguard the financial interests of taxpayers and of the town . . . A by-law . . . cannot be overridden at the behest of a majority of the voters present, in the absence of an article in the warrant under which such action can be taken." [109]

In the past there were a relatively large number of towns without by-laws. A three member commission appointed by the Governor prepared in 1920 a code of by-laws for towns as a model for towns without by-laws.[110] In 1940, the Massachusetts Federation of Taxpayers

[105] *Ibid.,* chap. 40, sec. 21.
[106] *Ibid.,* chap. 40, sec. 32.
[107] *Ibid.,* chap. 40, sec. 21.
[108] *Brown v. Town of Carlisle,* 336 Mass. 147 (1957).
[109] *Loring v. Inhabitants of Town of Westwood,* 237 Mass. 545 (1921).
[110] Commonwealth of Massachusetts, *Report of the Commission to Complete the Work of Revising and Codifying the Laws Relating to Towns,* Senate Number 2, 1920, pp. 38-42.

Associations, Inc. published a set of model by-laws to assist towns in updating their by-laws.[111] Today only ten towns have failed to adopt by-laws; all are small towns ranging in population from Gosnold (61) to Erving (1,353). Several towns have adopted only one by-law; Shutesbury (333) and Sunderland (1,298) each have adopted only a zoning by-law. Washington (298) has adopted only a by-law which provides for one week paid vacation and five paid holidays for employees of the highway department, and West Tisbury (389) has adopted one by-law authorizing the appointment of a finance committee and listing its duties.

Town by-laws often are out of print or in need of updating. Many town clerks are apologetic about the condition of the town by-laws and indicate a need for their revision by pointing to archaic provisions. Ashfield, for example, has one framed copy of its town by-laws which have not been amended since their adoption in 1849. Berlin has solved this problem by adopting a by-law requiring the selectmen to publish the by-laws at least once every five years.[112]

By-laws usually are printed as a separate pamphlet and paper supplements often are printed as new by-laws are adopted or old ones are amended. A few towns approach the publication of their by-laws in a different manner. Milton prints its by-laws in the annual town report; a practice to be commended as it is an inexpensive manner of making the by-laws readily available. It may not be essential to include the by-laws in each annual town report, but including them in the annual report every two or three years would be desirable. A case can be made for incorporating the by-laws and the warrant for the forthcoming annual town meeting in the annual town report as the provisions of the by-laws commonly regulate phases of town meetings.

Norwell binds its by-laws in a plastic cover and sells the pamphlet for two dollars and fifty cents; by-laws subsequently enacted are mailed to the purchasers for insertion, thereby keeping the by-laws up to date. Groton publishes a municipal manual for its citizens containing the by-laws of the town, legislative acts accepted, and other pertinent information bound in a three ring binder which facilitates adding or deleting pages.

---

[111] "Model By-Laws for Massachusetts Towns" (Boston: The Massachusetts Federation of Taxpayers Association, Inc., 1940).

[112] Berlin, Massachusetts, *By-Laws of the Town of Berlin*, art. I, sec. 3.

Special Districts

One of the least known phases of local government in Massachusetts is special district government within towns. Towns vary considerably in terms of geographical area, population, and population concentrations. It is not uncommon for a town to have two or more population clusters of unincorporated villages which require or desire services not needed elsewhere in the town. A governmental mechanism for the provision of services in one section of a town is the improvement district. A town meeting may authorize a village with a population of one thousand or more to organize an improvement district under a name approved by the meeting "for the purpose of erecting and maintaining street lamps, establishing and maintaining libraries, building and maintaining sidewalks, or for employing and paying police officers.[113] Each district must have a prudential committee and a clerk and may elect a treasurer and other officers; each district official holds office for one year or until a successor is qualified. A district is authorized to adopt by-laws to govern the calling of meetings and specify the duties of its officers.

Other special districts such as fire and water districts are created by special acts of the General Court which take effect when approved by a specified number, usually two-thirds, of the voters of the territory of the proposed district. For example, the General Court passed an act in 1933 to take effect when accepted by two-thirds of the voters within the territory of the district creating the West Boylston Water District of West Boylston as a corporate body, specifying the activities it may engage in, authorizing it to borrow money and hold district meetings, providing for a board of three water commissioners to hold office for three year terms, and authorizing the District to adopt by-laws.[114]

The government of a special district is basically the same as that of a town in terms of organization and procedures. The annual meeting of a special district is called by the issuance of a warrant by the prudential committee or governing board notifying the inhabitants of the district of where and when the meeting will be held and the articles to be acted upon; warrants are short and frequently contain only six to ten articles. Special meetings of the district may be called at the discretion of the governing board. Meetings of special districts are con-

---

[113] *Massachusetts General Laws,* chap. 40, sec. 44.
[114] *Massachusetts Acts of 1933,* chap. 352.

ducted in the same manner as town meetings. Fire, water, light, and improvement districts are authorized to elect by ballot at any annual election of district officers a moderator to preside at all district meetings held during the year.[115] Until a moderator or temporary moderator is elected, the district clerk presides and in his absence the chairman of the prudential committee presides.[116] The moderator of a district meeting performs the same functions as the moderator of a town meeting and in some towns the moderator of the town meeting is elected moderator of the special district meeting. The annual meeting of a special district utilizes select committees in the same manner as they are utilized by the annual town meeting. The Hyannis Fire District in 1963, for example, had two select committees: a Fire Station Site Committee and a Wage and Salary Committee. Attendance at meetings of a special district is less than at a town meeting as the district covers only a portion of the town and the number of important issues to be resolved is small. The governing board performs functions similar to those performed by selectmen of the town. The by-laws or rules and regulations of a special district are similar in nature to town by-laws.

An annual meeting of a water district, for example, will consider articles in the warrant dealing with the election of district officers, the appropriation of funds for salaries and operating expenses, borrowing money in anticipation of revenue, extension of water mains, creation of a stabilization fund, and installation of an automatic valve at the pumping station to stabilize water pressure. The annual meeting of a fire district will consider articles in the warrant dealing with the election of district officers, appropriation of funds for salaries and operating expenses, borrowing money in anticipation of revenue, entering into a contract with a water company for water service, purchase of new fire apparatus, transfer of money from the stabilization fund to the new apparatus fund, sale of a pumper, and purchase of land as a site for a new fire station.

---

[115] *Ibid.,* chap. 39, sec. 14.
[116] *Ibid.*

Chapter 3

The Representative Town Meeting

For three hundred years, the Massachusetts townsman has cherished his right to participate directly in the process of determining town policies and only reluctantly has agreed to the substitution of a representative policy determining mechanism for the open town meeting. Sentiment and tradition work against any change in the open town meeting.

The limited or representative town meeting is a hybrid political institution which seeks to combine certain features of the open town meeting with a representative body; the voters delegate legislative powers to a relatively large number of elected representatives, yet reserve the right to attend and speak at town meetings and by means of referenda reverse most actions of their elected representatives.

Origin

The date of the origin of the concept of a representative town meeting as a substitute for the open town meeting cannot be determined with precision. Dissatisfaction with the traditional form of town government manifested itself in Boston as early as 1708 when the selectmen reported that by-laws were not being properly executed for "the want of a proper head or Town officer or officers impowered for that purpose" and urged the appointment of a committee to draft a charter of incorporation for the town.[1] The town meeting held on December 27, 1708 voted that such a committee be chosen, but the March 14, 1709 town meeting rejected the report of the committee.[2]

Town records indicate the open town meeting functioned adequately albeit tumultuously on occasion for at least its first century and one half in all towns. It was not until the 1780s that rumblings of discontent with the plenary meeting as the local legislative body began to develop in Boston as its population increased.

---

[1] Boston, Massachusetts, *A Report of the Record Commissioners of the City of Boston, Containing the Boston Records from 1700 to 1728* (Boston: Rockwell and Churchill, 1883), p. 55.

[2] *Ibid.*, pp. 56-59.

51

Acting upon the petition of a large number of citizens that the sense of the town be taken on the question of the expediency of transforming the town of Boston into an incorporated city, a town meeting held in Fanuiel Hall on May 11, 1784 voted the appointment of a thirteen member committee headed by Samuel Adams to consider whether the form of government should be altered.[3]

On June 4, 1784, the committee reported two plans for a municipal corporation: The first plan provided for "incorporating the Town of Boston into a Body Politic by the Name, Style and Title of the Mayor, Aldermen and Common-Council of the City of Boston" and the second plan provided "for incorporating the Town of Boston into a Body Politic, by the Name, Style and Title of the President and Selectmen of the City of Boston." A town meeting held on June 17, 1784 rejected the plans by a great majority.[4]

An article representing the views of a considerable number of citizens was inserted in the warrant for a town meeting held on December 30, 1791 and called for the appointment of a twenty-one member committee to consider "the Present State of the Town;" the meeting approved the appointment of the committee.[5] It reported on January 13, 1792 a plan authorizing the selectmen to divide the town into nine wards of equal population and each ward annually to elect by ballot two voters residing in the ward who together with the selectmen would constitute a "Town Council" possessing the power to make "all such By Laws as the Town have now in their corporate capacity A right to make and establish the same . . . and to alter and repeal them."[6] The town council would have been authorized to appoint all executive officers except the selectmen, town clerk, overseers of the poor, assessors, town treasurer, school committee, auditors of account, firewards, collector of taxes, and constables.[7] This plan was defeated on January 26, 1792 by a vote of 701 to 517.[8]

On May 12, 1803, the Boston town meeting voted that a committee be organized to inquire into the affairs of Suffolk County; the committee reported on December 21, 1803 and on January 2, 1804 a

---

[3] Boston, Massachusetts, *A Volume of Records Relating to the Early History of Boston Containing Boston Town Records, 1784 to 1796* (Boston: Municipal Printing Office, 1903), p. 25.

[4] *Ibid.*, p. 42.

[5] *Ibid.*, p. 272.

[6] *Ibid.*, p. 274.

[7] *Ibid.*

[8] *Ibid.*, p. 275.

committee of twenty-four, two from each ward, was elected "to procure any alteration in the County and Town Government."[9] The report of the committee, dated February 29, 1804, was received by a town meeting held on March 12, 1804 which adjourned until April 9, 1804 at which time the report was read and the meeting after considerable debate voted to dissolve itself.[10]

The committee recommended a town council, composed of the selectmen and two delegates elected in each ward, be created with the power "to make all such Bye-Laws, Ordinances, Rules and Regulations, for the orderly government of the Town, and for the management of its concerns, as they may judge necessary."[11]

On October 16, 1815, a committee which considered the question of altering the town government reported to the town meeting that it rejected the concept of a city government, but urged a chief executive called "The Intendant" and a change in name to "The Intendant and Municipality of the Town and City of Boston."[12]

The committee advanced succinct arguments against the open town meeting in large towns which have a familiar ring today.

> It is impossible that all the individuals of which they are composed, should be well acquainted with the principles on which depend the prosperous conduct of the monied concerns of a corporation, and with those other subjects of internal regulation, by which the prosperity of a city is increased, and by which it is best enabled to encourage & protect the industry of its own citizens. If all the inhabitants of such towns assemble, it is obvious that business cannot be well transacted by so numerous a body, liable as it always must be, to be swayed by local views, party feelings, or the interests of designing men: If the meetings be, as it most frequently will be, but thinly attended, those present must act as the representatives of the whole; and it is very seldom, that men of the best intelligence and most capable of conducting publick business will leave their important private concerns to attend to affairs in which they have only a general interest; it therefore unavoidably happens that the affairs of a large town are conducted by a very small number of persons, who represent and act for the whole, but who are not chosen by them, who do not possess their confidence and act under no, or a very slight responsibility.[13]

[9] Boston, Massachusetts, *A Volume of Records Relating to the Early History of Boston Containing Boston Town Records, 1796 to 1813* (Boston: Municipal Printing Office, 1905), pp. 153-54.

[10] *Ibid.,* pp. 159-60.

[11] Boston, Massachusetts, *Report of the Town Convention,* February 29, 1804, pp. 1-2.

[12] Boston, Massachusetts, *A Volume of Records Relating to the Early History of Boston Containing Boston Town Records, 1814 to 1822* (Boston: Municipal Printing Office, 1906), pp. 38-42.

[13] *Ibid.,* p. 43.

The committee added that "all great bodies of men" including state governments, banking institutions, and corporations are managed by representatives or directors who "act for the joint interest under general laws." [14] A bill drafted by the committee provided that the selectmen, twenty-four delegates of whom two would be elected in each ward, and the "Intendant" would be "a body corporate & Politic" with power to adopt by-laws and ordinances. The "Intendant" was to be elected annually by the joint ballot of the selectmen, delegates, overseers of the poor, and the board of health and with the concurrence of the selectmen was to be responsible for the faithful execution of laws. [15]

By a vote of 950 to 920 the meeting refused to accept the report of the committee. [16] It appears that the chief reason for the rejection of the plan was the lack of a constitutional provision authorizing the General Court to incorporate city governments. No variation in the traditional form of town meeting government was allowed under the 1780 Constitution of the Commonwealth. The Second Amendment to the Constitution, adopted in 1821, empowered the General Court to establish limited town meetings in towns with a population in excess of 12,000 upon the application of and with the consent of a majority of the electorate at a town meeting called for the purpose. The 12,000 population figure appears to have been selected as a compromise as figures as high as 30,000 and as low as 5,000 had been considered.

A committee appointed on October 22, 1821 to consider "A complete system relating to the administration of Town and County" reported on December 10, 1821. The town meeting voted to recommit the report to the committee which was enlarged by the addition of one person from each ward and instructed "to report a system of Municipal Government for this town." [17]

The committee reported on January 2, 1822 and urged a city government, but proposed:

> That general meetings of the citizens, qualified to vote in City affairs, may from time to time be held, to consult upon the common good, to give instructions to their Representatives, and to take all lawful measures to obtain a redress of any grievances, according to the right secured to the people, by the Constitution of this Commonwealth. That such meetings shall be duly warned

[14] *Ibid.*
[15] *Ibid.*, pp. 45-46.
[16] *Ibid.*, p. 48.
[17] *Ibid.*, p. 254.

54

by the Mayor and Aldermen, upon the requisition of fifty qualified voters of said city.[18]

In 1822, Boston, with a population in excess of 43,000, abandoned
the town form of government in favor of a city charter because of
attendance problems. Faneuil Hall was overcrowded when a controversial article was on the warrant and only voters near the moderator
could hear the deliberations. When routine articles composed the warrant only the selectmen and thirty or forty other voters were present
and acted upon the articles and reports which the majority had not
carefully considered.

Role of Alfred D. Chandler

The institutional history of the representative town meetings in
Massachusetts is traceable to 1915. Alfred D. Chandler of Brookline
is considered the father of the representative town meeting as he first
attempted to persuade Brookline to adopt the plan at the end of the
nineteenth century and was successful in 1915. Newport, Rhode
Island, in 1906, became the first community to adopt the equivalent
of a representative town meeting when it amended its city charter to
provide for a council of one hundred and ninety-five members.

Brookline was experiencing difficulties with its open town meeting
late in the nineteenth century at which time Mr. Chandler advanced
the concept of a representative town meeting as an alternative to the
city form of government. To secure adoption of a representative town
meeting, Alfred D. Chandler had to overcome the firmly established
beliefs that every town voter had the right to participate fully in town
meetings and the representative town meeting would weaken or de-
stroy grass roots democracy. Fear also was expressed that citizen
apathy would be multiplied by the adoption of the representative town
meeting as citizens would become convinced there is no logical reason
to attend town meetings as they would have no voice in the decision
making process. In fact, relatively few non-town meeting members attend representative town meetings.

In response to a petition filed by a citizen group organized by Mr.
Chandler, the General Court in 1915 enacted a law authorizing the
question of the adoption of a representative town meeting to appear
on the ballot in Brookline.[19] Brookline voters adopted the plan by a

---

[18] *Ibid.,* pp. 256-59.
[19] *Massachusetts Special Acts of 1915,* chap. 250.

vote of 3,191 to 1,180.[20] Watertown adopted a representative town meeting acceptance statute on November 4, 1919.

The granting of woman suffrage in 1920 doubled the pressure for the abandonment of the open town meeting. Twelve towns accepted and Wakefield rejected representative town meeting acceptance statutes during the 1920s, thirteen towns accepted and three towns rejected acts during the 1930s, three towns accepted and Palmer rejected acts during the 1940s, and eleven towns accepted and Wakefield rejected acts during the 1950s. During the 1960s, Southbridge rejected a representative town meeting act and Montague accepted one.

Interest in the representative town meeting among several towns with a population under 12,000 led to the adoption in 1926 of the Seventieth Amendment which amended the Second Amendment by empowering the General Court to establish representative town meetings in towns with a population in excess of 6,000. Only three representative town meeting towns currently have a population under 12,000; Amesbury (11,617), Athol (11,989), and Montague (8,629). Sixty open town meeting towns ranging in population from Ashland (8,698) to Wakefield (25,571) are larger than the smallest town with a representative town meeting, Montague (8,629).[21]

The desirability of restricting representative town meetings to towns with a population in excess of 6,000 is questionable. Logically, a requirement of a prescribed minimum population to be eligible to have a representative town meeting has no validity. If the voters prefer a representative town meeting, they should be free to adopt it. Furthermore, the number of registered voters is of greater significance than the population of a town and the restriction of representative town meetings to towns with a population in excess of 6,000 has led to the paradoxical situation in which two towns eligible to adopt a representative town meeting have fewer registered voters than an ineligible town: Orange had a 1965 population of 6,206 and 2,945 registered voters and Templeton had a population of 6,006 and 2,579 registered voters, whereas Rockport had a population of 5,297 and 3,006 registered voters.

---

[20] Brookline, Massachusetts, *Town Report*, 1915, p. 74.
[21] Commonwealth of Massachusetts, *The Decennial Census 1965* (Boston: Secretary of the Commonwealth, 1965), pp. 5-7.

Reasons for Adoption

Four major reasons have been advanced in support of the adoption of the representative town meeting. First, a large town lacks the facilities to accommodate all voters. The number of registered voters exceeds by several times the capacity of the largest hall in the town and the use of two or more halls connected to the same public address system is cumbersome and less than satisfactory. Even a large attendance in one hall restricts the amount of genuine deliberation. Surprisingly, this reason appears to have little validity; most towns which adopted the representative town meeting did so because they had experienced quorum problems with the open town meeting except when the warrant contained an exceptionally controversial article.

To cite only two examples, Auburn had difficulty in attracting a quorum of fifty voters prior to the adoption of the representative town meeting and Athol in 1956 sounded the fire alarm at the town hall in an attempt to attract a quorum; the alarm was an attraction but citizens did not go into the meeting in sufficient numbers to establish a quorum.

Second, the conduct of an open town meeting with several thousand voters in attendance is difficult if not next to impossible. Only the failure of large numbers of voters to attend in the larger towns has prevented meetings from becoming unwieldy.

Third, the unrepresentativeness of the open town meeting in larger towns can be a serious problem. The representative town meeting substitutes legal representation for chance or accidental representation. The small attendance of registered voters at the typical open town meeting permits a minority group to pack the meeting and control town policies; a neighborhood sporadically will turn out in large numbers and vote appropriations for expensive capital improvements for the neighborhood. The conclusion is inescapable that a *de jure* representative town meeting provides better representation for all voters than a *de facto* representative town meeting.

Fourth, it is argued that town meeting members become well educated with respect to town problems and, consequently, are better prepared than the average citizen to vote intelligently on the articles in the warrant; conclusions also can be reached with less difficulty.

Legal Procedures for Adoption

Neither the Constitution of the Commonwealth of Massachusetts nor the General Court authorized towns by their own action to adopt a representative town meeting until the home rule constitutional Amendment was ratified in 1966.

Prior to 1966, a town wishing to adopt a representative town meeting voted at a town meeting to authorize the drafting and filing of a petition in the General Court requesting the enactment of a special act providing for a representative town meeting and making the act effective upon its acceptance by the town.

A special state commission reviewed the representative town meeting in 1931 and drafted a standard representative town meeting bill which was enacted by the General Court the same year.[22] Any town which accepted a special act providing for a representative town meeting may adopt the standard representative town meeting act. To date, only Arlington and Brookline have adopted the standard act.[23]

The standard and special representative town meeting acts are fundamentally the same; the details such as the number of members and ex officio members vary considerably from town to town. Most special acts were copied from earlier special acts. All acts contain ephemeral provisions which should be left to by-law determination.

The home rule constitutional Amendment authorizes towns to create a charter commission which may draft a new charter or amendment for submission to the voters for their action. Hopefully, a charter commission will not copy *ad verbatim* the provisions of a special representative town meeting statute which has been accepted by another town.

Nomination and Election of Members

The standard representative town meeting act provides for the division of the town into precincts by the selectmen and the special acts provide for the division of the town into precincts by the selectmen or others specified in the acts. Town meeting members are elected by non-partisan ballots from among the registered voters of each precinct and serve as delegates at the town meeting.

---

[22] *Massachusetts General Laws*, chap. 43A.

[23] Arlington and Brookline adopted the standard act on March 4, 1935 and March 10, 1942, respectively.

Twenty-three special acts specify a minimum and maximum number of precincts, seven acts specify a minimum number of precincts, the Framingham and Ludlow acts specify the number of precincts, and the remaining acts leave the number of precincts to by-law determination. Twenty-six acts establish a minimum number of voters in each precinct. Thirteen acts stipulate that each precinct shall have an approximately equal number of voters. The standard act does not stipulate the number of precincts, but does stipulate that each precinct must contain at least four hundred voters. A general law enacted in 1966 requires towns with a population in excess of 5,000 to revise decennially precincts to "contain, as nearly as can be ascertained, an equal number of voters."[24]

Experience clearly indicates it is preferable for town by-laws rather than the acceptance statute to specify the number of precincts and the number of voters in each precinct. If a limitation is incorporated in the act relative to the size of the representative town meeting, it would be preferable to limit the number of town meeting members rather than the number of voters per precinct.

Candidates for town meeting members are nominated by petitions which bear no political party designations; the required number of signatures of precinct voters on nomination petitions varies from ten in most towns to thirty in Milford. Ten signatures should be sufficient on a nomination petition as barriers preventing voters from becoming candidates should be kept to a minimum.

An incumbent in most towns automatically is renominated if he submits his written intention to seek re-election to the town clerk at least thirty days prior to the election. Fourteen special acts specify that the words "candidate for re-election" must be printed on the ballot under the names of incumbents seeking re-election. Re-election of incumbents is nearly automatic in every town. The designation "candidate for re-election" is undesirable as it grants an unfair advantage to incumbents and eliminates potential candidates who know it is difficult to defeat an incumbent who is so labelled on the ballot.

Forty-one towns elect town meeting members in March; Saugus elects its town meeting members on the first Tuesday after the first Monday of November of odd numbered years. All representative town meeting acts provide that town meeting members are the judges of the election and qualifications of their members who receive no compensation for their service.

---

[24] *Massachusetts General Laws*, chap. 54, sec. 9A.

Number and Term of Elected Members

The number of elected town meeting members ranges from fifty in Saugus to three hundred and eighty-four in Fairhaven. The most common number is in the neighborhood of two hundred and forty; this number has been selected in emulation of the two hundred and forty members of the House of Representatives of the General Court.

With the exceptions of Framingham and Saugus, the representative town meeting is a continuing body; one-third of the town meeting members are elected each year for a three year term. Framingham and Saugus elect all town meeting members simultaneously for a two year term.

The acceptance statute either stipulates the total number of elected town meeting members or specifies the formula to be used in determining the number of elected members. The Adams acceptance statute, for example, provides that the number of town meeting members in each precinct shall "consist of the largest number divisible by three which will admit of a representation of all precincts by an equal number of members and which will not cause the total elected town meeting membership to exceed one hundred and fifty."[25] The Amherst act stipulates that one town meeting member shall be elected for every twenty registered voters in each precinct and the Winthrop act restricts the number of elected town meeting members in each precinct to the largest number divisible by three which is less than three per cent of the registered voters in the precinct.

The standard representative town meeting act stipulates the "membership shall in each precinct consist of the largest number divisible by three which will admit of a representation thereof in the approximate proportion which the number of registered voters therein bears to the total number of registered voters in the town, and which will cause the total membership to be as nearly 240 as may be."[26]

In the typical town the number of women who serve as town meeting members is relatively small: three to ten per cent of the total membership. Many women town meeting members serve only one term and do not seek re-election.

---

[25] *Massachusetts Acts of 1935,* chap. 235, sec. 2.
[26] *Massachusetts General Laws,* chap. 41A.

Vacancies

A town meeting member may resign by filing a written notification of resignation with the town clerk which is effective upon filing. A member automatically vacates his office by moving from the town. If he moves to another precinct, he continues to hold office until the next annual town election.

Most acts stipulate that a vacancy may be filled until the next annual election by the remaining members of the precinct from among the voters thereof. However, the Agawam, Auburn, Dedham and Shrewsbury acts provide that a vacancy is filled by the unsuccessful candidate who received the most votes provided he consents to serve.

The number of vacancies caused by resignations is apparent upon examination of the ballot in a typical town; in each precinct the voters are instructed to vote for one or more candidates for a one or two year term to fill vacancies.

Ex Officio Members

Representative town meeting statutes with the exceptions of Framingham, Montague, Saugus, and Swampscott designate or authorize the town to designate by by-law specified town officers as members ex officio to participate in the meeting as members at large. Although Athol is authorized to designate ex officio members by by-law, it has not done so.

The standard representative town meeting act authorizes the town by by-law to designate ex officio members and this is preferable to statutory designation as it introduces flexibility instead of rigidity in the procedure for designating ex officio members. The Amherst and Easthampton statutes specify a number of officials as ex officio members and authorize the designation of other town meeting members at large by by-law.

The number of ex officio members varies from none in five towns to thirty-five in West Springfield. As a courtesy most representative town meeting statutes extend ex officio membership to any member of the General Court residing in the town. The actual number of ex officio members in a town varies annually with changes in membership in the General Court and the number of town offices held by an individual entitling him to ex officio membership.

The theory behind ex officio membership for key town officials is to ensure their presence at town meetings. The importance of having major town officials present at representative town meetings is apparent, yet the desirability of designating them ex officio members is questionable as they undoubtedly would attend meetings as non-members and have the same right as other non-town meeting members to speak. Furthermore, they are eligible to serve as elected town meeting members.

No serious arguments have been advanced against the practice of having members at large provided the number of such members is small. Opponents of a large number of ex officio members approve the designation of the moderator, town clerk, selectmen, and chairman of the finance committee as ex officio members, but oppose extending the list for fear that an administrative bloc with its better sources of information would control the meeting.

The Athol representative town meeting act resolves the problem of attendance of key town officials by stipulating "it shall be the duty of the chairman of each board or committee of the town, elected or appointed, and the head of each department to attend throughout that part of each town meeting at which matters other than those to be acted upon and determined by ballot are to be considered."[27]

The designation by statute or by-law of specified town officials as ex officio members of the representative town meeting apparently is of no great consequence as it is not unusual for ex officio members to be elected town meeting members by the voters of their precincts. The town clerk in Belmont, for example, is both an ex officio and an elected member of the representative town meeting. It is common practice in towns where few or no town officers are designated as ex officio members for the officers to be elected in their precincts as town meeting members.

Town Employees as Town Meeting Members

A subject of controversy is whether paid town employees should be allowed to serve as elected town meeting members. It occasionally is maintained that town employees dominate town meetings and vote themselves higher wages and shorter working hours.

Robert J. Tilden has written "it is not expected that voting trends in meetings will divide strictly along employment lines. The significant

---

[27] *Massachusetts Acts of 1954*, chap. 382, sec. 6.

point is that many issues are carried or lost by a few votes. Every decision reached by a margin which is less than the size of the 'employee bloc' is immediately suspect. If the issue involves employee wages or benefits the vote is *prima facie* a result of self interest. What the outcome would be if such a vote were tested in the courts is an interesting question."[28]

Should the representative town meeting not represent the wishes of the town on matters of wages and working hours, the disgruntled citizens may initiate corrective action by a petition for a referendum and at future annual town meetings elect new town meeting members to replace incumbents who do not represent the majority views of the town. Only citizen apathy can allow paid town employees to dominate a town meeting and citizen action is the proper corrective.

A Framingham study committee investigated the charge that town employees serving as town meeting members would vote as a bloc and control the meeting; the committee concluded "there was no merit to the belief that town employees were exerting any great influence on the meeting."[29]

A survey of the representative town meeting towns and an examination of their records fail to reveal town meetings dominated by town employees. The consensus among close observers of representative town meetings is that town employees serving as town meeting members do not dominate the meetings and as taxpayers and citizens have the right to seek election as town meeting members.

The proposal has been made on numerous occasions that paid town employees should be made legally ineligible to serve as town meeting members. Whether the General Court possesses the constitutional power to disbar town employees from service as elected town meeting members is debatable and has not been resolved by the courts. It has been pointed out that the General Court has forbidden city employees to serve on a city council.

Agreement has been reached on one point: The General Court may forbid a town employee serving as an elected town meeting member to vote on articles which personally affect him. Interestingly, the code of ethics adopted by the General Court in 1962 specifically exempts elected town meeting members from its provisions.[30]

---

[28] Robert J. Tilden, "Separation of Powers and the Representative Town Meeting," *Massachusetts Law Quarterly*, March, 1957, p. 28.

[29] Framingham, Massachusetts, *Report of the Committee Studying Changes in the Town Government* (Framingham: March, 1965), pp. 14-15.

[30] *Massachusetts General Laws*, chap. 268A, sec. 1(g).

Precinct and Pre-Town Meeting Meetings

In a few towns all precincts are organized, a precinct chairman is elected, and meetings attended by town meeting members and voters of each precinct are held to discuss the articles in the warrant for a forthcoming town meeting. Members of the finance committee usually attend the precinct meetings to explain the committees recommendations.

The Agawam representative town meeting statute directs the town clerk annually to call a meeting of the town meeting members prior to June first to organize by precincts by electing a chairman and secretary for a one year term.[31] The chairman must call a meeting of the town meeting members and voters of the precinct at least seven days prior to a town meeting for the purpose of discussing the warrant. If the chairman fails to call the meeting, it may be called by any three town meeting members. The secretary is instructed to maintain a town meeting attendance record for inclusion on the annual report of the town. The Agawam finance committee attends precinct meetings, but the turnout of town meeting members and citizens has been disappointing.

Auburn has a by-law which provides that one town meeting member in each precinct is charged with the duties of keeping town meeting members informed and calling them for meetings. The Auburn Representative Town Meeting Review Committee in 1963 recommended establishing a "cadre" of town meeting members from each precinct to promote attendance at town meetings and help educate the members. The committee suggested that a copy of the finance committee's report be mailed with the warrant to each town meeting member. Furthermore, sponsors of articles and others possessing special knowledge of articles should prepare and transmit reports to the members.[32]

The finance committee, League of Women Voters, taxpayers association, town meeting members association in Danvers, or other organization sponsors a pre-town meeting meeting to which town meeting members and voters are invited. In Belmont, for example, the League of Women Voters holds four simultaneous pre-town meeting meetings; two precincts are invited to each meeting.

---

[31] *Massachusetts Acts of 1955,* chap. 632, sec. 9.

[32] Auburn, Massachusetts, *Report of the Representative Town Meeting Review Committee* (Auburn: January 14, 1963).

Attendance at pre-town meeting meetings commonly is slight and questions are raised as to their value in view of the fact town meeting members commonly ask the same questions at town meetings as are raised at the pre-town meeting meetings.

Powers and Procedures of the Representative Town Meeting

The representative town meeting possesses all powers of an open meeting *ad referendum*. The acceptance statutes empower the representative town meeting to act for and bind the town by stipulating "all powers vested in the municipal corporation so far as conforms with the provisions of law now or hereafter applicable to the transaction of town affairs and town meetings shall, when taken by any representative town meeting in accordance with the provisions of this act, have the same force and effect as if such action had been taken in a town meeting by the voters of the town."

Procedures

A representative town meeting is called and conducted in the same manner as an open town meeting with one exception: Only town meeting members may vote. The selectmen call the meetings by the issuance of a warrant at least seven days prior to each meeting. The Supreme Judicial Court rendered an advisory opinion that "it is within the competency of the General Court to enact a law which would provide for the conducting of a representative town meeting . . . because the Selectmen unreasonably refuse to call a town meeting."[33] In the event the selectmen unreasonably refuse to call a town meeting, a justice of the peace upon the written petition of one hundred registered voters or ten per cent of the registered voters may call a meeting by issuing a warrant and notice must be given to town meeting members as provided by law.[34]

Representative town meetings are holding longer sessions with the passage of time. Framingham, for example, had eleven adjourned sessions to complete action on the warrant for the 1964 annual meeting. The increasing length of the warrant in the larger towns

[33] *Opinion of the Justices to the House of Representatives,* 347 Mass. 792 (1964).
[34] *Massachusetts General Laws,* chap. 39, sec. 12.

apparently has resulted in hasty action on certain articles in order to conclude the meeting. The selectmen in several towns place the most important and controversial articles at the beginning of the warrant to ensure that they receive proper consideration while attendance is high; this practice is to be commended.

The town clerk is charged with the responsibility of notifying the members of a town meeting. He is required to give members at least seven days notice with the exception of four towns; five days notice is required in Falmouth and Wellesley and three days notice is required in Milton and South Hadley.

With the exception of Saugus, the moderator is popularly elected at the annual town meeting for a term of one or three years and serves until his successor is elected and qualified. In Saugus the moderator is elected by the representative town meeting from its membership. The Supreme Judicial Court ruled in 1940 that the powers granted by statute to the moderator to preside and preserve order at town meetings are unaffected by the adoption of the limited or representative town meeting.[35] In the absence of the moderator, town meeting members are authorized to elect a moderator pro tempore. Commonly, all motions are required to be in writing. In Needham the moderator expedites action at town meetings by mailing to each town meeting member prior to a meeting a letter stating that he as moderator considers certain specified articles routine and urges each member to review the warrant prior to the town meeting "to determine those articles which should be adopted unanimously without debate."

In spite of an Arlington by-law providing for the use of *Robert's Rules of Order,* the Supreme Judicial Court held that a town which had accepted the standard representative town meeting act could amend its by-laws by a majority vote regardless of the provision in *Robert's Rules* that a majority vote of the entire membership would be necessary.[36]

Several acceptance statutes forbid the meeting to delay indefinitely action upon an article. For example, the Agawam statute provides "no article in the warrant shall at any representative town meeting be finally disposed of by a vote to lay upon the table, to indefinitely postpone, or by other dilatory action."[37]

---

[35] *Doggett v. Hooper,* 306 Mass. 129 (1940).
[36] *Blomquist v. Town of Arlington,* 338 Mass. 594 (1959).
[37] *Massachusetts Acts of 1955,* chap. 632, sec. 8.

The Framingham annual town meeting on March 11, 1964 adopted a code of ethics for debate patterned after the Massachusetts conflict of interest law.

> *ARTICLE FIRST:* Any person who is employed as an attorney, engineer, architect, land surveyor, broker, employee or in any other capacity by another interested in the Article under discussion shall disclose his or her employment before speaking thereon.
>
> *ARTICLE SECOND:* Any person who has a financial interest in the Article under discussion shall disclose his or her financial interest before speaking thereon.
>
> *ARTICLE THIRD:* Any person who is the spouse, parent, child, brother or sister of a person who has a financial interest in the Article under discussion shall disclose such relationship before speaking thereon.
>
> *ARTICLE FOURTH:* A Town Meeting Member shall have the right to raise a "point of order" and request that the Moderator inquire of the speaker whether he or she has an interest in the Article required to be disclosed by the rules of Town Meeting and if the speaker has such an interest, why it was not disclosed before speaking on the merits of the Article.

The Framingham meeting rejected a section of the proposed code which would have required any person speaking on an appropriation article to disclose "his or her vocation or principal type of employment."

Quorum. The 1915 Brookline act established a majority of the town meeting members as the quorum. A similar quorum requirement has been established by the standard representative town meeting act and all but five of the special acceptance statutes. Belmont, Fairhaven, Framingham, Lexington, and Watertown have established less than a majority as the quorum. A number of town meeting members less than a quorum is authorized to organize temporarily and adjourn from time to time.

It is ironic that a system designed specifically to overcome the quorum problem and unrepresentativeness of the open town meeting should experience similar problems. The adoption of less than a majority as the quorum requirement clearly is undemocratic and opens the door for a disciplined minority to control the town. One purpose of establishing a representative town meeting was to substitute a system of *de jure* representation for a system of *de facto* representation determined by chance. The interests of the majority are placed in jeopardy by a quorum requirement of less than a majority. The preferable approach to the solution of the quorum problem is the reduction of the size of the representative town meeting.

Secret Ballots. Towns are authorized by general law to enact by-laws regulating proceedings at town meetings, and a representative town meeting by a two-thirds vote may use secret ballots.[38] The Stoughton representative town meeting act, however, was amended in 1960 by stipulating that all votes must be taken by standing vote or voice.[39]

Whether secret ballots should ever be used in a representative town meeting is a subject of considerable controversy. The Associated Fire Fighters of Massachusetts, AFL-CIO in 1961 introduced a bill forbidding the use of secret ballots at representative town meetings which was amended to allow the use of secret ballots if two-thirds of the town meeting members voted to authorize their use; the bill was vetoed by the governor.[40] In a veto message, dated February 27, 1961, returning a similar bill, Governor John A. Volpe stated:

> The question as to whether a town should require a two-thirds vote or any other percentage to have a secret ballot is not the issue. The important and traditional right of home rule and self government in the Towns of the Commonwealth should not be interfered with and it is my sincere belief and opinion that the people of each Town should have the right as they presently do under existing statutes, to adopt such by-laws and parliamentary procedure as best meets the needs of their respective Towns. This bill, if signed by me, would violate the time honored custom of home rule.[41]

An amendment to the general laws enacted in 1963 provides that secret ballots may not be utilized unless their use is authorized by a two-thirds vote of the town meeting members present.[42]

The Massachusetts Selectmen's Association, Inc. introduced in 1965 a bill requiring all votes on all bond issues be by roll call vote, but the General Court referred the bill to the next annual session, a technique utilized to kill a bill without directly voting to do so.[43]

Advocates of the use of secret ballots on highly controversial articles maintain a secret ballot is a mechanism which protects town meeting members from possible reprisals by town employees, neighbors, and others. According to a study committee, the non-use of secret ballots in towns such as Framingham has resulted in the re-

---

[38] *Massachusetts General Laws,* chap. 39, sec. 15.
[39] *Massachusetts Acts of 1960,* chap. 394.
[40] *Massachusetts House No. 2345,* 1961.
[41] *Massachusetts House No. 2790,* 1961.
[42] *Massachusetts Acts of 1963,* chap. 320.
[43] *Massachusetts House No. 2240,* 1965.

luctance of a significant number of town meeting members to vote on important articles.[44] It also is maintained that the absence of a secret ballot provision would decrease the number of candidates for town meeting members as businessmen would hesitate to seek office for fear of losing customers and other citizens may fear incurring the wrath of their employers.

Although the arguments in favor of the use of secret ballots have a certain amount of validity, elected representatives can be held responsible and their performance evaluated only if they vote publicly. As a delegate a town meeting member cannot be forced to vote on a particular article according to the dictates of his constituents, but is obligated to inform them of his vote.

A survey of twenty-five representative town meeting towns in 1940 revealed that there was no by-law providing for secret ballots in sixteen towns; in six towns secret ballots were used when a majority of the town meeting members voted to use them; in Ludlow secret ballots were used if the vote was questioned by seven voters or the moderator was in doubt after a second show of hands; in Fairhaven secret ballots were used if a motion to use them was supported by twenty-five town meeting members and was made prior to the vote; and in Dartmouth secret ballots were used on the demand of forty town meeting members.[45]

A survey of the forty-two representative town meeting towns in 1964 and 1965 disclosed that secret ballots seldom were used; twenty-six towns reported secret ballots were not used and the remaining towns indicated secret ballots had been used on rare occasions in the past.

Referendum

The voters in accepting a representative town meeting act did not foresake all policy determining powers; every act grants voters power with a few exceptions to veto actions taken at a representative town meeting by means of a protest referendum. Direct democracy can override representative democracy.

The provisions for referenda in the acts vary. In many towns a referendum may be held on any action of the representative town meeting, but in other towns the use of the referendum is restricted

---

[44] Framingham, Massachusetts, *Report of the Committee Studying Changes in the Town Government,* p. 14.

[45] "Representative Town Meetings in Massachusetts," p. 21.

to actions appropriating funds in excess of a specified amount. The standard representative town meeting act allows a referendum to be held on any vote appropriating in excess of twenty thousand dollars, establishing a new board or town office, fixing the term of office of town officials if the term is optional, increasing or decreasing the number of members of a board, and adopting or amending a by-law.[46] To cite only one other example, Amherst voters are precluded from utilizing the referendum to reverse actions of the representative town meeting appropriating less than five thousand dollars or money to pay maturing bonds or notes, or authorizing borrowing in anticipation of taxes, or a vote passed by two-thirds of the members as an emergency measure to preserve the peace, health, safety, or convenience of the town.[47] If citizens are to control policies, a referendum should be permitted to reverse all actions of the town meeting except actions necessitated by bone fide emergencies.

Procedure

With the exceptions of certain actions specified in the acceptance statute, no vote taken at a representative town meeting becomes effective until a specified number of days, five to ten excluding Sundays and holidays, have elapsed in order to permit circulation of petitions calling for a protest referendum. The specified period for filing a referendum petition commences with the dissolution of the town meeting regardless of the number of adjourned sessions held subsequent to the vote in question. Opponents of an action taken by a representative town meeting may collect signatures prior to the dissolution of the meeting.[48]

The procedure for holding a referendum is initiated by the filing of a petition signed by a specified number of registered voters. In fifteen towns the required signatures—ranging from one hundred to five hundred—may be collected on a town-wide basis. In nineteen towns the number of signatures required is expressed in terms of a specified percentage of the registered voters of the town—three to five per cent of the registered voters. In eight other towns the specified number or percentage of signatures must be obtained in each precinct.

---

[46] *Massachusetts General Laws,* chap. 43A, sec. 10.
[47] *Massachusetts Acts of 1936,* chap. 10, sec. 8.
[48] *Hinch v. Lindsey,* Essex Superior Court Docket No. 103390 (1955).

The Greenfield act specifies that a referendum petition must be signed by at least two hundred voters or fifty town meeting members.[49]

The standard representative town meeting act permits a referendum if three per cent of the registered voters sign petitions within five days of the dissolution of the meeting; a majority vote in the referendum reverses the action of the representative town meeting provided the majority is composed of at least twenty per cent of the registered voters.[50] The Watertown and Winchester acts also specify that the representative town meeting vote is not reversed unless the majority voting to reverse is composed of at least twenty per cent of the registered voters. The stipulation of a majority composed of at least twenty per cent of the registered voters is desirable as it ensures that there is substantial town support for the reversal of the representative town meeting action and prevents a small minority which lost at the representative town meeting from winning its point in a referendum in which participation may be slight.

Recision of a representative town meeting action by the voters in a referendum does not preclude the representative town meeting from adopting a similar or identical article in a warrant for a subsequent meeting.

In drafting a representative town meeting charter provision, it clearly is preferable to express the number of signatures required to initiate a referendum in terms of a fixed percentage of the registered voters. The required percentage should not be so low that it encourages referenda on most actions of the town meeting, but should not be so high that it effectively prevents dissatisfied citizens from collecting the required number of signatures. Three to five per cent of the registered voters would appear to be a reasonable requirement.

To ensure that there is town-wide support for a referendum, a provision could be incorporated in the act requiring that a specified per cent of the voters in each precinct must sign the petition; if this is done, the precinct requirement should be lower in terms of a percentage of the registered voters than the town-wide requirement. The provision might stipulate that a referendum may be initiated by a petition signed by three per cent of the registered voters provided at least one per cent of the voters in each precinct sign the petition.

Considering the number of controversial issues resolved by representative town meetings, it is surprising there have been so few refer-

---

[49] *Massachusetts Acts of 1921,* chap. 440, sec. 8.
[50] *Massachusetts General Laws,* chap. 43A, sec. 10.

71

enda. Sixteen of the forty-two towns with representative town meetings have never had a referendum. In most of the remaining towns referenda are uncommon and the representative town meeting usually is upheld by the referenda. In general, the voters tend to be more economically minded than the town meeting members and reverse the vote of the representative town meeting authorizing large expenditures.

Committees

The Saugus and Swampscott representative town meeting statutes direct the moderator to appoint a finance committee consisting of one town meeting member from each precinct. In Norwood by custom the moderator usually restricts committee membership to town meeting members.

A Shrewsbury town government study committee in 1965 recommended the creation of committees of town meeting members on the grounds that all legislative bodies utilize a committee system and members would become thoroughly familiar throughout the year with the town functions assigned to the jurisdiction of their respective committees. The study committee suggested that the following committee be organized and composed of town meeting members: finance, streets and sidewalks, sewers, water, police department, fire department, public buildings, education, legislative matters, recreation, planning and zoning, electric power and light, personnel, public health, claims, and by-laws.[51]

The study committee recommended that committee members be appointed by the moderator and each town meeting member should serve on at least one committee; each precinct would have equal representation on each committee. To provide continuity, the study committee suggested that two members of each of the six precincts should serve on each committee. "A system of representation among the various committees with promotion from the less important to those of major importance might well serve to broaden the town meeting members' knowledge and sustain interest in town meeting government."[52]

At least one department head in Shrewsbury opposes committees of town meeting members on the ground they would encroach upon

---

[51] Shrewsbury, Massachusetts, *Report of Town Government Study Committee* (Shrewsbury: 1965), p. 8.
[52] *Ibid.*

the prerogatives of the town manager to the point that the department heads no longer would have one superior as they currently do under the town manager system; a new body would be interposed between the manager and the department heads. Others believe that existing boards and commissions such as the sewer commission, light commission, and planning board can function better than committees of town meeting members who would work for improvements in their own precincts rather than for the overall good of the town. In other representative town meeting towns the consensus is the belief that committees of town meeting members would duplicate the work of the finance committee or usurp its function. A possible compromise would be the creation of a finance committee, as in Saugus and Swampscott, composed exclusively of town meeting members.

To be realistic, it is highly improbable that committees of town meeting members would play an active role in town government if the attendance of town meeting members at special town meetings is a reliable index of the amount of time town meeting members are willing to devote to town affairs.

Chapter 4

The Town Meeting: An Evaluation

Twentieth century political observers generally criticize the New England town meeting and conclude it has outlived its usefulness. Nevertheless, no Massachusetts town has abandoned the town meeting in favor of a city council during the past forty-four years. Although critics may attribute the remarkable tenacity of the town meeting to myopic townsmen, a judicious appraisal of the town meeting as the local legislature leads to different conclusions.

The Open Town Meeting

The open town meeting is the oldest political institution in two hundred and seventy Massachusetts towns — more than three and one-third centuries old. With continued urbanization and concomitant problems of unprecedented magnitude doubts have arisen concerning the ability of the open town meeting to function adequately and survive in the second half of the twentieth century.

It has been fashionable in recent years to attack the open town meeting as undemocratic in practice and to question its ability to resolve space age problems. An editorial in a national publication in 1965 stated the town meeting "still lingers on as an instrument of control by small groups of self-seekers and without participation by 90 per cent of the eligible voters."[1] And the Committee for Economic Development in 1966 criticized the open town meeting by stating it "met the needs of simpler earlier times, but was not designed to handle the complex modern problems confronting rapidly growing areas."[2]

The New England town meeting form of local government is not without its advantages and in the minds of many is a venerable institution possessing a mystic quality where "pure" democracy flourishes. In contrast to twentieth century criticism, nineteenth century political observers praised the town meeting.

---

[1] "The Fading Town Meeting," *National Civic Review,* October, 1965, p. 522.
[2] *Modernizing Local Government* (New York: Committee for Economic Development, July 1966), p. 30.

Alexis de Tocqueville wrote: "The New Englander is attached to his township . . . because it constitutes a strong and free body of which he is a member, and whose government claims and deserves the exercise of his sagacity . . . The existence of the townships of New England is in general a happy one. Their government is suited to their tastes, and chosen by themselves . . . the commotions of municipal discord are unfrequent. The conduct of local business is easy."[3]

Lord Bryce wrote: "Of the three or four types of systems of local government which I have described, that of the town or township with its primary assembly is admittedly the best. It is the cheapest and the most efficient; it is the most educative of the citizens who bear a part in it. The Town Meeting has been not only the source but the school of democracy."[4]

All venerable political institutions should be re-examined periodically to determine their viability and whether they deserve to survive. Are the eulogies of the open town meeting deserved or folklore? Is the New England town meeting a viable example of "pure" democracy or a degenerate descendant of a formerly great institution of local government? Does poor attendance and relative lack of debate constitute its syndrome? Is the town meeting devoid of merit and "a sacred cow that deserves to be laid to rest"?[5] Has population growth and the development of megalopolis undermined the *raison d'etre* of the town meeting?

A plethora of seemingly plausible evidence has been marshalled by vociferous critics to document the deficiencies of the open town meeting and to label it an anachronism. One of the difficulties with the evidence which makes the evaluation of the open town meeting as an effective political institution difficult is the fact that the towns with open town meetings differ substantially from one another in many respects although the basic governmental structure is the same. Furthermore, the number of empirical studies of individual town meetings is small.

The experience of two hundred and seventy Massachusetts towns with open town meetings suggests that the critics are attacking this

---

[3] Alexis de Tocqueville, *Democracy in America,* 3rd American ed. (New York: George Adlard, 1839), pp. 62-63.

[4] James Bryce, *The American Commonwealth,* 2nd ed. rev., Vol. I (London: Macmillan and Co., 1891), p. 591.

[5] John W. Alexander and Morroe Berger, *"Is the Town Meeting Finished?" The American Mercury,* August, 1949, p. 151.

form of government by evaluating it against an idealized version conjured up in their minds which has never existed in actuality or are evaluating it in terms of their subjective views of what it should be. The twin problems of poor attendance and relative lack of debate are the two major charges hurled against the open town meeting.

Attendance Problems

Citizen apathy is a common charge against town meeting government and the charge cannot be denied if town meeting attendance in the typical town is an accurate barometer of such apathy. Attendance at the annual meeting which acts on many important subjects including the town budget is small unless the warrant contains one or more "hot" issues; it is not unusual for less than ten per cent of the registered voters to make the formal decisions. Special town meeting attendance is sparse if the warrant contains only routine articles and the meeting may have to be adjourned for lack of a quorum if held during the summer months.

For sundry reasons, a large percentage of the registered voters voluntarily abdicate power which is rightfully theirs and their nonattendance at an open town meeting may be interpreted as a vote of confidence in a *de facto* representative town meeting which may or may not, in fact, be representative. Fortunately, attendance appears to be a function of the importance of the unresolved issues; apathy disappears when a major one is brought to the town meeting for resolution. And there is little evidence that the *de facto* representative town meeting consistently thwarts the general will.

Attendance figures today, compared to those of early town meetings, appear to document the charge that citizens have become apathetic. It must be recognized, however, that attendance of seventeenth century freemen was compulsory and absentees were fined. Whether those freemen were disinterested and lethargic is a moot question. Furthermore, the freemen constituted only a small percentage of the total population of early Massachusetts towns. Those who attend town meetings today are interested and usually reasonably well informed citizens. The quality of town government would not be improved by compelling apathetic and indifferent voters to attend and participate in town meetings. To criticize the open town meeting on the ground of the failure of all voters to participate is to base criticism on an unrealistic norm.

Lord Bryce wrote that attendance at town meetings was generally good during the latter half of the nineteenth century.[6] Several reasons account for the decline in attendance. The numerous problems encountered by rapidly growing towns have lengthened the warrant and the meeting, thereby producing voter fatigue. As the evening drags on, voters gradually leave the hall as action is completed on items with the greatest interest. Many do not wish to devote the required time to town affairs; often, the annual meeting requires multiple sessions over a period of a week or more to consider and act upon all articles.

The annual town meeting has ceased to be a holiday and pageant in all but the smallest towns. It no longer performs the social functions it did because the increased length of the warrant leaves no time for a town meeting dinner and other social gatherings. It appears to be safe to assume that a number of citizens were more interested in the social functions than the issues to be resolved at the town meeting. The entertainment attraction of the town meeting also has declined. The increased length of the meeting undoubtedly has decreased attendance by necessitating tighter parliamentary control; towns no longer can afford the luxury of allowing the meeting to be conducted as a vaudeville show for the entertainment of the citizenry as used to be the case in certain towns. The town meeting today generally is orderly and not obstreperous and tumultuous as in the past in a number of towns.

"Commuteritis" is a problem in suburban towns; many voters are tired by the time they return home from work in the evening. A related development contributing to low voter participation is the greater mobility of citizens. New voters may have no strong attachment to the town and believe they are not well enough acquainted with the candidates and issues to vote intelligently. Television undoubtedly is a culprit at least partially responsible for the attendance problem at town meetings. When a choice has to be made between the town meeting and one or more favorite television programs the town meeting is apt to be the loser as far as a significant number of voters are concerned, especially if the warrant contains only non-controversial articles.

The reduction in attendance is to be lamented, yet it generally has not had a debilitating effect on the open town meeting and may be attributed in part to refinements in procedures which result in the resolution of most issues prior to the town meeting. The finance com-

---

[6] Bryce, *The American Commonwealth*, p. 566.

mittee, which developed in the latter part of the nineteenth century as a valuable adjunct of the town meeting, brings expert talents to bear on local problems. It is the Argus or watchdog of town finances and, in most towns, studies and reports on all warrant articles. A significant number of citizens are content to rely upon this committee to provide adequate advice to the town meeting and, hence, rationalize there is no need to attend the meeting. A similar reliance is placed in many towns upon the planning board to provide proper advice to the town meeting on zoning and other planning matters.

In approximately one-half of the towns the finance committee, League of Women Voters, or other civic association sponsors a "pre-town meeting meeting" at which the finance committee's report is presented and discussed. These meetings are not always well attended, yet they, along with the printed report of the committee and press coverage, afford the electorate the opportunity to study issues, reach conclusions, and agree on compromises prior to the actual meeting. When this process has taken place, many citizens rationalize that their presence is not required at the meeting, particularly if a popular television program is scheduled for the same evening.

In the larger towns, only the absence of a significant number of voters makes it possible for the meeting to function with reasonable efficiency. If all voters attempted to attend, no auditorium would accommodate the crowd and the meeting would function with difficulty in two or three large auditoriums connected by an intercommunications system. Efforts to increase attendance in these towns, if successful, would necessitate the adoption of a representative town meeting or another form of government.

With respect to the "attendance problem" of the open town meeting, an important question which needs answering is whether low citizen participation is a basic fact of political life in any form of local government. A related question is whether effective local government is dependent upon general citizen participation.

Town Meeting Debate

Early towns were small, problems were relatively few, diversions were limited in number, and adequate time was available for genuine deliberations at the town meeting. These circumstances rarely prevail today. The amount of debate at town meetings varies from town to town and year to year depending in large measure upon the number of unresolved issues. Copious oratory generally is a thing of the past. In certain towns the population is relatively homogeneous and a consensus on solutions to problems has been achieved; town meeting proceedings are decorous. Occasionally, the consensus breaks down and debate becomes acrimonious. In other towns where the population is more heterogeneous, battle lines on major issues are sharply drawn and considerable pungent debate takes place.

The amount of debate at town meetings in general, however, has declined. At the typical town meeting, business is dispatched perfunctorily and swiftly, relatively few in the audience speak, and articles commonly are passed as recommended by the finance committee unanimously with little or no debate. The impression is given that complicated issues have not been fully debated. To an outsider, the meeting may appear to be a relatively dull ratification assembly and the erroneous conclusion may be drawn that no serious debate has taken place.

The reduction in the amount of debate at town meetings is partially attributable to refinements in government procedures which result in the resolution of most issues prior to the meeting. It is not surprising that the average attendee tends to rely upon the recommendations of the finance committee, whose members commonly are lawyers, businessmen, engineers, and other professionals, and hesitates to criticize the report of a committee which has been studying the issues during the past year or longer. It is not unusual after a period of debate to hear a voter say, "Why are we wasting time? We have high-caliber people on the finance committee who have the best interest of the town in mind. We should accept their recommendations."

There is conflict in varying degrees in every town, but the quantity of town meeting debate is not always a reliable index of the degree of conflict. The veil of decorum at the town meeting may be hiding factional differences. The relative absence of pointed debate does not necessarily mean that the town is strongly united. The "pre-town meeting meeting" and informal gatherings which discuss town issues also contribute to the reduction of debate at town meetings as many issues were thoroughly debated prior to the town meeting. And the minority may have concluded it was useless to contest the issues again and, consequently, may boycott the town meeting.

Competence of the Town Meeting

Certain critics concede that town meetings were competent to solve the simple problems which confronted a rural society in the seventeenth and eighteenth centuries, but contend many issues which come before a space-age town meeting are so highly complex and technical they are beyond the ability of the average citizen to resolve intelligently.[7] Are inordinate demands being made upon the voters? Is the guidance of experts a necessity? Town meetings today rely more heavily than in the past upon experts for guidance on technical matters and this has reduced the amount of town meeting deliberation. The role of the town meeting participant is becoming limited on technical questions more and more to choosing which expert to rely upon for advice.

Robert C. Wood, in commenting upon the town meeting, contends that "an excessive reliance on direct popular action can lead . . . to no popular action at all with the citizens baffled and perplexed and the expert and the small clique in charge."[8] Any person who has attended several town meetings in various towns would be forced to disagree with this contention. Inaction on major issues in towns is no more common than in cities. Admittedly, there is an increased tendency to defer to the expert on baffling issues, yet the town meeting retains ultimate power and does not always defer to the expert. His advice on a technical question may be rejected if the town meeting does not accept his logic; the meeting also may decide it needs more time to familiarize itself with the issue and, therefore, postpones definitive action. Experts will testify from experience that they have not usurped the functions of the open town meeting; its unpredictability is proverbial.

Disregard of Procedural Requirements

Robert C. Wood has written:

> The most significant feature of small town politics is the frequency with which legal and procedural requirements are overlooked and ignored. They are always to be adjusted according to the "common sense, down-to-earth judgment" of the participants, to take account of unique conditions and provincial peculiarities. Tickets can be fixed, favors granted, contracts awarded, not because these irregularities will remain hidden but because they are acceptable on the basis of personal esteem. The successful town moderator is the one who moderates between the rules of the game and the disposition of the meeting.[9]

---

[7] *Modernizing Local Government*, p. 30.
[8] Robert C. Wood, *Suburbia: Its People and Their Politics* (Boston: Houghton Mifflin Company, 1959), p. 284.
[9] *Ibid.*, pp. 278-79.

Although Wood does not refer specifically to the Massachusetts town, one is apt to conclude that moderators in Massachusetts towns overlook or ignore legal and procedural requirements. This is untrue; evidence of moderators not following procedural requirements is completely lacking. A moderator with the consent of the meeting may conduct the meeting informally rather than formally, but this does not mean that procedural requirements are discarded. Further, the moderator will conduct the meeting strictly by the book if the informal method of conducting the meeting encounters difficulties. Massachusetts town moderators are men of demonstrated ability and in a large per cent of the towns are lawyers whose profession recognizes the importance of observing procedural requirements.

The Representative Town Meeting

The theory of the representative town meeting for large towns is supported by logic, yet the representative town meeting has been beset by major and minor problems in many towns. It has not been the panacea for the problems of the open town meeting that had been anticipated in 1915 when Brookline abandoned the open town meeting. On the other hand, the representative town meeting generally has functioned adequately and no serious attempt has been made to abandon it in any town.

The lack of candidates for town meeting member in certain precincts in most towns, quorum problems at special town meetings, and the relative lack of debate have disturbed students of town government.

Lack of Candidates

The number of candidates for the office of town meeting member is small and frequently is equal to, or less than, the number of town meeting members to be elected. Only on rare occasions are there two candidates for each position. The number of candidates would be even less except for the active recruitment of candidates by the town clerk and other town officials.

In 1964 and 1965, the total number of candidates for town meeting members exceeded the number to be elected, but in one town one precinct was one candidate short of its quota. In several towns the number of candidates in one or more precincts was precisely equal to the number of town meeting members to be elected.

Experience indicates that the number of candidates for town meeting members in most towns usually declines with the passage of time. Shrewsbury, in 1954 for example, had 349 candidates for 198 positions, but the number has dropped to approximately 250 candidates. It is unfortunate that a town, Shrewsbury for example, has experienced a shortage of candidates in certain precincts while contests in other precincts have resulted in citizens deeply concerned with town affairs failing to be elected town meeting members. A Shrewsbury town government study committee suggested in 1965 that "consideration be given to providing a method by which a deficiency in candidates for the office of town meeting members in one or more precincts may be compensated for by the election of a like number of members-at-large." [10]

The most commonly advanced proposal to solve the problem of the lack of candidates is a reduction of the size of the representative town meeting to increase the number of contests.

Ideal Size. Four problems must be resolved in determining the ideal number of elected town meeting members. First, the representative town meeting must not be of a size which would cause deliberative and procedural problems. The representative town meeting should be the smallest body which adequately represents the divergent opinions in the town and allows the greatest amount of genuine deliberation.

Second, the number of town meeting members to be elected in each precinct must not be so great as to place an inordinate burden upon voters to determine the candidates best qualified to hold office. Voting records indicate that the average voter in a precinct leaves part of the town meeting members section of the ballot blank. If the number of candidates is exactly equal to the number of vacancies to be filled, the voter may rationalize his vote will not change the results of the election. If he votes, he may vote only for the candidates he is personally acquainted with.

Third, the representative town meeting must not be of such size that the number of qualified candidates is insufficient in each precinct to ensure a contest for each office. The representative town meeting is in serious trouble if many offices are uncontested and citizens have to be begged or coerced into seeking public office as town meeting members.

---

[10] Shrewsbury, Massachusetts, *Report of the Town Government Study Committee* (Shrewsbury: April 2, 1965), pp. 7-8.

Fourth, the representative town meeting must not be of such size that quorum problems are encountered, especially at special town meetings.

The third and fourth considerations listed above are the resultant of citizen apathy and a statement that citizens should not be apathetic does not solve these problems. Hence, it is preferable to adjust the size of the representative town meeting to obviate any problems attributable to citizen apathy.

In 1945, the Massachusetts Federation of Taxpayers Associations, Incorporated suggested the following criteria for determining the most desirable size for a representative town meeting.

> First, that 240 elected members should be considered a *maximum* and that a smaller number does not possess any inherent disadvantage;
>
> Second, that while the number of town meeting members should perhaps bear a fixed relationship to the number of voters, this should not exceed one for every fifty registered voters in the smaller towns, should be somewhat less in most towns, and far less in the larger towns;
>
> Third, that the number of members from a single precinct should not exceed 15 or 5 to be elected each year.[11]

It is difficult to quarrel with these criteria; they are as valid today as they were when set down in 1945. Had towns followed these criteria, they would not be experiencing problems attracting candidates and quorums.

Attendance Problems

In theory, town meeting members should be more conscientious than townsmen in attending a town meeting as the former have accepted a civic responsibility by seeking public office. An Athol study committee reported in 1953:

> It would appear moreover that this form of town meeting places a definite responsibility upon certain of the citizens viz—the town meeting members to attend all of the town meetings and vote on the various articles in the warrant. There is no such fixed responsibility under the so-called open form of town meeting, where each voter follows his own personal inclination in the matter of attending.[12]

Nevertheless, the representative town meeting often has experienced attendance problems at adjourned sessions of the annual meeting and at special meetings.

---

[11] Representative Town Meetings in Massachusetts," (Boston: Massachusetts Federation of Taxpayers Associations, Inc., June 1945), p. 10.

[12] Athol, Massachusetts, *Report of the Committee "To Consider the Subject of a Representative Form of Town Government"* (Athol: May 15, 1963), pp. 4-5.

Attendance at the annual meeting usually is good if action is completed in one evening; attendance at adjourned sessions of the annual meeting dwindles. Too many town meeting members obviously are derelict in the performance of their duties.

The representative town meeting appears to operate most satisfactorily in terms of attendance during its early years when interest is high. With the passage of time, attendance declines. In Shrewsbury, attendance at the first session of the annual meeting has varied from ninety-eight per cent in 1954, the first representative town meeting, to seventy-six per cent in 1963. With the exception of a special meeting held on January 9, 1956 and attended by ninety per cent of the members, attendance at special meetings in Shrewsbury has declined from seventy-four per cent in 1954 to fifty-three per cent in 1963. The figures refer to the opening of the meeting which frequently commences one-half hour subsequent to the appointed hour in order to permit the securing of a quorum.[13] The reluctance of voters to seek election as town meeting members undoubtedly contributes to the attendance problem as certain members are disinterested and were persuaded to seek election.

Concern with the noticeable laxity of town meeting members to attend town meetings led to the appointment of a sub-committee of the Framingham Committee Studying Changes in the Town Government to work with the rules committee of the representative town meeting in attempting to solve the problem. Two resolutions were presented to town meeting members at a special town meeting held on January 12, 1964 and adopted: One requires the printing in a local newspaper a few days prior to the annual town election the attendance record of town meeting members during the previous two years and the second directs the rules committee to notify town meeting members who have failed to attend a majority of the meetings held during the previous two years.[14]

Many towns print the attendance record of town meeting members in the annual report of the town in the hope that they will be shamed into attending the meetings. Winthrop published the attendance record in the annual report and believed the system was working well until it was discovered that certain members were attending only long enough to have their presence recorded.

---

[13] Shrewsbury, Massachusetts, *Report of the Town Government Study Committee,* p. 2.

[14] Framingham, Massachusetts, *Report of the Committee Studying Changes in the Town Government* (Framingham: March 1965), p. 4.

In Connecticut, the town clerk calls a special meeting of the town meeting members from a precinct to vote on the question of declaring a seat vacant if the incumbent has failed to attend three consecutive meetings. This system merits serious consideration by Massachusetts towns which desire to retain relatively large town meetings. A related solution for the attendance problem would be a charter provision stipulating that the seats of town meeting members who fail to attend a specified number of successive meetings would be declared vacant by the moderator unless the members had legitimate reasons for the absences.

Quality and Quantity of Debate

The quality of debate at representative town meetings in general is superior to that which takes place at an open town meeting. Extraneous material and personalities seldom are interjected and, as one would anticipate, the average town meeting member is better informed than the average participant in an open town meeting, thereby raising the level of debate.

One complaint directed against the representative town meeting is the relative absence of debate and the number of town meeting members who attend but never or seldom participate in the debates. There are several explanations for the modicum of debate.

Debate tends to be limited when many issues have been settled prior to the town meeting as the result of pre-town meetings, informal meetings, and study and consideration of the finance committee's report. Certain town meeting members, especially newly elected ones, feel they are not sufficiently acquainted with the issues to participate in genuine debate; others believe their forensic ability is limited. Furthermore, a town meeting member often feels overwhelmed when presented with a town budget of several million dollars. Legally he possesses the power to approve, increase, or reduce the budget, but in practice feels powerless for the lack of independent and reliable information. He often feels he is not in a position to question seriously the recommendations of the finance committee which has been scrutinizing town finances over the past year and has examined critically the proposed budget.

It was hoped when the representative town meeting was developed that its members would complete the requisite amount of homework prior to town meetings. The questions asked and arguments advanced indicate that not all members arrive at the meeting adequately prepared to participate in genuine deliberation. Attendance at and advance preparation for all town meetings are prerequisites if town meeting members are to be better informed than the average townsman.

Non-Members. The forgotten men in representative town meeting towns are the non-town meeting members. Although they have the right to attend and speak at representative town meetings, few attend the typical meeting. Often only a newspaper reporter and one or two non-member citizens are present in addition to the town meeting members. The inclusion of a controversial article in the warrant is no guarantee that many citizens will attend although it increases the prospects that a large number will attend. Non-members seldom speak at representative town meetings. Clearly the representative town meeting does not perform the function of citizen education as well as the open town meeting.

Conclusions

The stereotypes of the town meeting advanced by its caustic critics often are a serious distortion of reality. That the open town meeting has its shortcomings cannot be denied, yet critics have been premature in sounding its knell. It apparently will continue to exist in many towns without necessarily appearing to be a dynamic institution.

Resistance to the abandonment of the open town meeting is strong: No Massachusetts town has abandoned the open town meeting in favor of a city charter since 1922 and only three towns have abandoned the open town meeting in favor of the representative town meeting during the past ten years. Sixty open town meeting towns, ranging in population from Ashland (8,698) to Wakefield (25,571), are larger than the smallest town with a representative town meeting, Montague (8,629).

Sentiment alone is not responsible for the persistence of the open town meeting. The Massachusetts townsman may be sentimental, but practical realities are of more importance to him. In general, townsmen appear to be convinced they can make decisions themselves as good as, or superior to, decisions that could be made by a body of elected representatives. In spite of the charges made against the open town meeting, local law-making appears to be functioning adequately and pungent critics have failed to present evidence that a city council or other alternative would exercise more sagacity in choosing solutions for town problems.

In retrospect, the open town meeting has proved to be a lithe and tenacious institution which demonstrates that government by mass meeting of interested citizens is still possible. It has coped successfully with serious problems in the past and should continue to do so until a town's population growth necessitates its abandonment in favor of a representative town meeting.

With respect to the representative town meeting, Professor William B. Munro prophesied in 1937 it was a step toward the ultimate: city government.

> The town meeting ceases to be a satisfactory organ of local government when the population of the towns exceeds five or six thousand. . . . For this reason many towns, on reaching an unwieldly size, apply for incorporation as cities . . . Others . . . have attempted to modify the town meeting without actually abolishing it, but these halfway measures do not seem to be proving altogether successful.
> The most common modification is to provide for a "limited town meeting." . . . This arrangement, however, is only a makeshift.[15]

Are the lack of candidates and associated attendance problems a portent of the future of the representative town meeting? One should not be too hasty in tolling the mourning bells for the representative town meeting. Empirical evidence supports the conclusion that it is firmly implanted. Townspeople appear to be generally satisfied with the representative town meeting as evidenced by the fact no town has ever voted to abandon it in favor of a city government or the open town meeting although articles have been inserted in warrants proposing the repeal of the system; article forty-nine of the warrant for the March 1954 Framingham annual town meeting, for example, proposed such a repeal. Furthermore, only Peabody, Westfield, and Gardner have abandoned the town form of government since 1915. And no town has become a city, but thirty-five towns have adopted the representative town meeting since 1922 when Gardner abandoned town government.

The representative town meeting is not a perfect instrument of representation, but neither is the alternative: a city council. The conclusion is inescapable that the representative town meeting is a mechanism which successfully has adapted town meeting government to the larger towns.

---

[15] William B. Munro, *The Government of the United States*, 4th ed. (New York: The Macmillan Company, 1937), pp. 743-44.

The town meeting may be a maladroit institution, yet it generally has resolved major town problems in a satisfactory manner. It is, of course, a truism that a city council can take faster action than a town meeting as town government procedures are designed to ensure that full and adequate consideration is given before action is taken. Consequently, town government theoretically may move more slowly than a city government in resolving pressing problems. Yet in actual practice town governments frequently initiate action to solve problems more expeditiously than cities.

In evaluating the Massachusetts town meeting, we should not make the error of placing the three hundred twelve towns in the same category; the multiformity of town institutions must be accorded recognition. Variety is as characteristic of Massachusetts towns as uniformity and each town should be evaluated separately in terms of meeting the needs of its citizens. Furthermore, the town meeting should not be judged on the basis of unrealistic standards.

The only general prognosis which may be advanced with validity is a mixed one. That town meeting government has problems must be admitted, yet it has been improving and is receptive to further improvement which will transform it into an even more effective legislative assembly.

Appendices

Appendix A

Massachusetts Towns

Population* and Governmental Features

1967

Town	Population*	Open Town Meeting	Representative Town Meeting	Executive Secretary to the Board of Selectmen	Town Manager
Abington	11,790	X			
Acton	10,188	X			
Acushnet	6,717	X			
Adams	12,703		X		
Agawam	17,484		X		
Alford	224	X			
Amesbury	11,617		X		
Amherst	10,097		X		X
Andover	20,551	X			X
Arlington	52,482		X		X
Ashburnham	3,042	X			
Ashby	2,089	X			
Ashfield	1,218	X			
Ashland	8,698	X			
Athol	11,989		X		
Auburn	15,396		X		
Avon	5,175	X			
Ayer	3,820	X			
Barnstable	15,609	X			
Barre	3,860	X			
Becket	876	X			
Bedford	10,787	X		X	
Belchertown	5,758	X			
Bellingham	10,604	X			
Belmont	28,794		X		
Berkley	1,769	X			
Berlin	1,984	X			

* *The Decennial Census, 1965* (Boston: Secretary of the Commonwealth, 1965)

1967

Town	Population*	Open Town Meeting	Representative Town Meeting	Executive Secretary to the Board of Selectmen	Town Manager
Bernardston	1,560	X			
Billerica	23,633		X		
Blackstone	6,025	X			
Blanford	859	X			
Bolton	1,669	X			
Bourne	6,376	X			
Boxborough	1,163	X			
Boxford	3,004	X			
Boylston	2,732	X			
Braintree	33,954		X		
Brewster	1,533	X			
Bridgewater	11,056	X			
Brimfield	1,644	X			
Brookfield	2,002	X			
Brookline	53,608		X	X	
Buckland	1,846	X			
Burlington	19,473	X			
Canton	15,310	X			
Carlisle	2,011	X			
Carver	2,147	X			
Charlemont	903	X			
Charlton	4,017	X			
Chatham	4,195	X			
Chelmsford	23,040	X			
Cheshire	2,718	X			
Chester	1,143	X			
Chesterfield	649	X			
Chilmark	300	X			
Clarksburg	1,945	X			
Clinton	13,626	X			
Cohasset	6,559	X			
Colrain	1,461	X			
Concord	14,516	X			X

* *The Decennial Census, 1965* (Boston: Secretary of the Commonwealth, 1965)

1967

Town	Population*	Open Town Meeting	Representative Town Meeting	Executive Secretary to the Board of Selectmen	Town Manager
Conway	948	X			
Cummington	602	X			
Dalton	7,360	X			
Danvers	24,764		X		X
Dartmouth	17,187		X	X	
Dedham	26,618		X		
Deerfield	3,481	X			
Dennis	4,374	X			
Dighton	4,131	X			
Douglas	2,718	X			
Dover	3,592	X			
Dracut	16,535	X		X	
Dudley	6,960	X			
Dunstable	1,021	X			
Duxbury	6,211	X			
East Bridgewater	7,460	X			
East Brookfield	1,788	X			
East Longmeadow	11,988	X			
Eastham	1,733	X			
Easthampton	12,974		X		
Easton	10,130	X			
Edgartown	1,513	X			
Egremont	1,013	X			
Erving	1,353	X			
Essex	2,502	X			
Fairhaven	15,642		X		
Falmouth	13,832		X		
Florida	679	X			
Foxborough	12,223	X			
Framingham	52,369		X	X	
Franklin	14,721	X			
Freetown	3,337	X			
Gay Head	113	X			

* *The Decennial Census, 1965* (Boston: Secretary of the Commonwealth, 1965)

95

1967

Town	Population*	Open Town Meeting	Representative Town Meeting	Executive Secretary to the Board of Selectmen	Town Manager
Georgetown	4,644	X			
Gill	1,290	X			
Goshen	437	X			
Gosnold	61	X			
Grafton	11,571	X			
Granby	4,770	X			
Granville	984	X			
Great Barrington	7,147	X			
Greenfield	18,265		X		
Groton	4,500	X			
Groveland	4,866	X			
Hadley	3,568	X			
Halifax	2,637	X			
Hamilton	6,141	X			
Hampden	3,211	X			
Hancock	517	X			
Hanover	7,862	X			
Hanson	5,285	X			
Hardwick	2,395	X			
Harvard	2,360	X			
Harwich	4,830	X			
Hatfield	2,708	X			
Hawley	249	X			
Heath	300	X			
Hingham	17,576	X			
Hinsdale	1,485	X			
Holbrook	11,231	X			
Holden	11,504	X			X
Holland	798	X			
Holliston	8,915	X			
Hopedale	4,363	X			
Hopkinton	5,512	X			
Hubbardston	1,365	X			

* *The Decennial Census, 1965* (Boston: Secretary of the Commonwealth, 1965)

1967

Town	Population*	Open Town Meeting	Representative Town Meeting	Executive Secretary to the Board of Selectmen	Town Manager
Hudson	13,642	X			
Hull	8,836	X			
Huntington	1,454	X			
Ipswich	9,955	X		X	
Kingston	4,946	X			
Lakeville	3,773	X			
Lancaster	4,815	X			
Lanesborough	3,062	X			
Lee	6,021	X			
Leicester	8,701	X			
Lenox	4,661	X			
Leverett	976	X			
Lexington	31,388		X	X	
Leyden	343	X			
Lincoln	4,463	X		X	
Littleton	5,572	X			
Longmeadow	13,809	X			
Ludlow	15,922		X		
Lunenburg	7,321	X			
Lynnfield	9,821	X			
Manchester	4,386	X			
Mansfield	8,620	X			X
Marblehead	20,942	X			
Marion	3,481	X			
Marshfield	10,176	X			
Mashpee	665	X			
Mattapoisett	3,942	X			
Maynard	9,070	X			
Medfield	7,479	X			
Medway	6,869	X			
Mendon	2,310	X			
Merrimac	3,733	X			
Methuen	32,466		X		

* *The Decennial Census, 1965* (Boston: Secretary of the Commonwealth, 1965)

1967

Town	Population*	Open Town Meeting	Representative Town Meeting	Executive Secretary to the Board of Selectmen	Town Manager
Middleborough	11,726	X			X
Middlefield	280	X			
Middleton	3,909	X			
Milford	17,034		X		
Millbury	10,764	X			
Millis	5,262	X			
Millville	1,706	X			
Milton	27,708		X	X	
Monroe	213	X			
Monson	7,324	X			
Montague	8,629		X		
Monterey	580	X			
Montgomery	397	X			
Mount Washington	53	X			
Nahant	4,067	X			
Nantucket	3,714	X			
Natick	30,365		X		
Needham	29,303		X		
New Ashford	174	X			
New Braintree	530	X			
New Marlborough	1,103	X			
New Salem	449	X			
Newbury	3,485	X			
Norfolk	3,985	X			
North Andover	12,514	X			
North Attleborough	15,682	X			
North Brookfield	3,608	X			
North Reading	9,882	X			
Northborough	8,314	X			
Northbridge	11,502	X			
Northfield	2,412	X			
Norton	6,737	X			
Norwell	6,387	X			

* *The Decennial Census, 1965* (Boston: Secretary of the Commonwealth, 1965)

Town	Population*	Open Town Meeting	Representative Town Meeting	Executive Secretary to the Board of Selectmen	Town Manager
Norwood	28,978		X		X
Oak Bluffs	1,492	X			
Oakham	632	X			
Orange	6,206	X			
Orleans	3,181	X			
Otis	572	X			
Oxford	10,034	X			
Palmer	11,394	X			
Paxton	2,856	X			
Pelham	921	X			
Pembroke	7,708	X			
Pepperell	4,573	X			
Peru	220	X			
Petersham	990	X			
Phillipston	842	X			
Plainfield	261	X			
Plainville	4,252	X			
Plymouth	15,424		X		
Plympton	1,060	X			
Princeton	1,487	X			
Provincetown	3,463	X			X
Randolph	21,726		X	X	
Raynham	5,937	X			
Reading	21,188		X		
Rehoboth	5,489	X			
Richmond	1,121	X			
Rochester	1,693	X			
Rockland	15,054	X			
Rockport	5,297	X			
Rowe	276	X			
Rowley	2,862	X			
Royalston	739	X			
Russell	1,514	X			

* *The Decennial Census, 1965* (Boston: Secretary of the Commonwealth, 1965)

1967

Town	Population*	Open Town Meeting	Representative Town Meeting	Executive Secretary to the Board of Selectmen	Town Manager
Rutland	2,713	X			
Salisbury	4,032	X			
Sandisfield	614	X			
Sandwich	2,438	X			
Saugus	23,429		X		X
Savoy	303	X			
Scituate	14,458	X			
Seekonk	9,880	X			
Sharon	11,341	X		X	
Sheffield	2,355	X			
Shelburne	1,819	X			
Sherborn	2,333	X			
Shirley	3,180	X			
Shrewsbury	18,003		X		X
Shutesbury	333	X			
Somerset	15,080	X			
South Hadley	14,249		X		
Southampton	2,634	X			
Southborough	4,780	X			
Southbridge	19,384	X			
Southwick	5,619	X			
Spencer	8,514	X			
Sterling	3,711	X			
Stockbridge	2,417	X			
Stoneham	20,109	X			
Stoughton	19,686		X		X
Stow	3,191	X			
Sturbridge	4,006	X			
Sudbury	10,894	X		X	
Sunderland	1,298	X			
Sutton	3,921	X			
Swampscott	13,995		X		
Swansea	11,767	X			

* *The Decennial Census, 1965* (Boston: Secretary of the Commonwealth, 1965)

Town	Population*	Open Town Meeting	Representative Town Meeting	Executive Secretary to the Board of Selectmen	Town Manager
Templeton	6,006	X			
Tewksbury	18,079	X			
Tisbury	2,080	X			
Tolland	104	X			
Topsfield	4,375	X			
Townsend	3,990	X			
Truro	962	X			
Tyngsborough	3,848	X			
Tyringham	251	X			
Upton	3,502	X			
Uxbridge	8,265	X			
Wakefield	25,571	X		X	
Wales	757	X			
Walpole	16,390	X			
Ware	7,886	X			
Wareham	10,406	X			
Warren	3,578	X			
Warwick	438	X			
Washington	298	X			
Watertown	40,115		X	X	
Wayland	12,192	X		X	
Webster	14,357	X			
Wellesley	26,297		X	X	
Wellfleet	1,651	X			
Wendell	294	X			
Wenham	3,114	X			
West Boylston	6,057	X			
West Bridgewater	5,731	X			
West Brookfield	2,233	X			
West Newbury	2,049	X			
West Springfield	26,070		X		
West Stockbridge	1,337	X			
West Tisbury	389	X			

* *The Decennial Census, 1965* (Boston: Secretary of the Commonwealth, 1965)

1967

Town	Population*	Open Town Meeting	Representative Town Meeting	Executive Secretary to the Board of Selectmen	Town Manager
Westborough	10,567	X			
Westford	8,283	X			
Westhampton	723	X			
Westminster	4,452	X			
Weston	9,848	X		X	
Westport	8,200	X			
Westwood	12,123	X		X	
Weymouth	50,468		X		
Whately	1,127	X			
Whitman	12,373	X			
Wilbraham	9,707	X			
Williamsburg	2,389	X			
Williamstown	7,042	X			X
Wilmington	15,261	X			X
Winchendon	6,689	X			
Winchester	21,634		X		
Windsor	430	X			
Winthrop	20,398		X		
Worthington	643	X			
Wrentham	7,517	X		X	
Yarmouth	8,715	X			

* *The Decennial Census, 1965* (Boston: Secretary of the Commonwealth, 1965)

Appendix B

Warrant for the 1963 Annual Town Meeting of Brookline, Massachusetts

THE COMMONWEALTH OF MASSACHUSETTS

Norfolk, ss.

To any Constable of the Town of Brookline, Greetings:

In the name of the Commonwealth of Massachusetts, you are hereby required to notify and warn the inhabitants of the Town of Brookline qualified to vote in elections to meet at the polling places designated for the several precincts in the said town on Tuesday, the Fifth Day of March, 1963, at seven o'clock in the forenoon for the following purpose, to wit:

To choose by ballot the following Town Officers:

Two Selectmen ....For three years
Treasurer ....For three years
Three Members of the School Committee ....For three years
Four Trustees of the Public Library ....For three years
Two Trustees of the Walnut Hills Cemetery ....For three years
One Member of the Brookline Housing Authority ....For five years
One Member of the Brookline Redevelopment
    Authority ....For five years

also

Seven Town Meeting Members ....For three years
    In Precincts 1, 2, 3, 4, 5, 6, 7, 8, 9, 10, 11 and 12
Two Town Meeting Members ....For two years
    To fill vacancies in Precinct 12
One Town Meeting Member ....For two years
    To fill vacancy in Precincts 1 and 11
Three Town Meeting Members ....For one year
    To fill vacancies in Precinct 8
One Town Meeting Member ....For one year
    To fill vacancy in Precincts 2, 4, 5, 9 and 12

Also for the purpose of giving their "Yes" or "No" on the following questions:

QUESTION No. 1

"Shall an act passed by the General Court in the year nineteen hundred and sixty-three entitled 'An Act establishing a department of public works in the Town of Brookline exercising the powers of certain other departments and Town offices,' be accepted?"

YES	
NO	

QUESTION No. 2

"Shall an act passed by the General Court in the year nineteen hundred and sixty-three entitled 'An Act establishing a park and recreation commission in the Town of Brookline,' be accepted?"

YES	
NO	

QUESTION No. 3

"Shall the public water supply for domestic use in the Town be fluoridated?"

YES	
NO	

QUESTION No. 4

"Shall the Town extend contributory group hospital, surgical and medical insurance to elderly persons retired from the services of the Town and to their dependents with fifty per cent of the premium cost and a portion of the administrative expense to be paid by the Town?"

YES	
NO	

QUESTION No. 5

"Shall the Town purchase additional Group Life and Group Accidental Death and Dismemberment Insurance for employees in accordance with the provisions of Chapter 32B of the General Laws with no contribution by the Town?"

YES	
NO	

For these purposes the polls will be open at seven o'clock in the forenoon and shall be closed at eight o'clock in the afternoon.

And in the name of the Commonwealth, you are further required to notify and warn the said Inhabitants to meet at the High School Auditorium in said Town on Tuesday, the Twenty-sixth Day of March, 1963, at seven-thirty o'clock in the evening for the following purposes to wit:

FIRST ARTICLE. — To see if the Town will vote that the number Measurers of Wood and Bark be two, to be appointed by the Selectmen.

SECOND ARTICLE. — To see if the Town will authorize the Treasurer, with the approval of the Selectmen, to borrow money from time to time in anticipation of the revenue of the financial years beginning January 1, 1963 and January 1, 1964 and to issue a note or notes therefor, payable within one year, and to renew any note or notes that may have been given for a period of less than one year, in accordance with Section 4 of Chapter 44 of the General Laws as amended.

THIRD ARTICLE. — To see if the Town will amend Article I-B of the By-Laws of the Town by adding, deleting or substituting positions or classes in the Classification Plan, or will otherwise amend said Article I-B.

FOURTH ARTICLE. — To see if the Town will amend the Pay Plan by establishing, deleting or substituting minimum, maximum or flat rate salaries for any position or class which may have been added to, deleted from or substituted in the Classification Plan under the preceding article; or by changing any of the existing salaries; or by amending the general provisions with respect to sick leave, vacation leave and the like; or will otherwise amend said Pay Plan.

FIFTH ARTICLE. — To see if the Town will accept the provisions of Chapter 520 of the Acts of 1962 (General Laws, Chapter 41, Section 108F) entitled, "An Act Establishing a Minimum Annual Compensation for Firefighters in Certain Cities and Towns."

SIXTH ARTICLE. — To see if the Town will vote to amend the Pay Plan by increasing the wages by 15% of all employees under the Classification and Pay Plans.

SEVENTH ARTICLE. — To see if the Town will accept Chapter 561 of the Acts of 1960 entitled, "An Act Allowing Cities and Towns to Enter into Collective Bargaining Agreements."

EIGHTH ARTICLE. — To see if the Town will amend Article I-B of the By-Laws of the Town by reallocating the following positions to the following higher grades and salaries.

PATROLMAN, from Grade X ($109.00) to Grade XIII ($121.50)

POLICE SERGEANT, from Grade XIII ($124.50) to Grade XVI ($141.50)

POLICE LIEUTENANT, from Grade XVI ($141.50) to Grade XVIII ($158.00)

POLICE CAPTAIN, from Grade XVIII ($158.00) to Grade XX ($175.00)

or will otherwise amend said Article I-B.

NINTH ARTICLE. — To act upon the appropriations asked for or proposed by the Selectmen or by any other officer, board or committee, and to fix the salary or other compensation of all elected officers of the Town as provided in Section 108 of Chapter 41 of the General Laws, as amended.

TENTH ARTICLE. — To see if the Town will raise and appropriate the sum of one hundred twenty thousand, five hundred dollars ($120,500) for the installation, making of connections, and housing of equipment for the fluoridation of the water supply of the Town.

ELEVENTH ARTICLE. — To see if the Town pursuant to the provisions of Section 95A of Chapter 32 of the General Laws will grant an annuity to the survivors specified in said section, of any deceased official or employee who died or was retired or pensioned under the circumstances set forth in said section, and will determine the amount of any such annuity within the limitations imposed by said section.

TWELFTH ARTICLE. — To see if the Town will authorize the transfer of ninety thousand dollars ($90,000) from the funds allotted to the Town by Chapter 782 of the Acts of 1962 entitled, "An Act Relative to the Accelerated Highway Program," and to appropriate the sum of ninety thousand dollars ($90,000) to permit the reconstruction, repair and resurfacing of certain public ways within the Town.

106

THIRTEENTH ARTICLE. — To see if the Town will raise and appropriate the sum of seventy thousand, nine hundred and sixty dollars ($70,960) to be expended by the School Committee, with the approval of the Board of Selectmen, for the purchase of furniture, furnishings and equipment for the new John D. Runkle School, or will take any other action with respect thereto.

FOURTEENTH ARTICLE. — To see if the Town will raise and appropriate the sum of twenty-five thousand dollars ($25,000) to be expended by the School Committee, with the approval of the Board of Selectment, for the preparation of preliminary plans for additions and alterations to the High School, or will take any other action with respect thereto.

FIFTEENTH ARTICLE. — To see if the Town will amend the Building Code as follows:

1. To amend the last sentence of Article 1, Section 104b. to read as follows: The elevator inspectors shall have had at least five years' experience in charge of the installation of elevators and moving stairways or be building inspectors duly qualified by the Division of Civil Service to inspect elevators.

2. To amend the clause in the first sentence of Article 5, Section 503-2a following the words, "except as follows" to read as follows: Walls separating apartments in buildings of Division B-2 Occupancy shall be of 2-hour fire resistive construction and walls enclosing apartments in Type 4 buildings shall be of at least 1-hour fire resistive construction.

3. To amend Article 5 by inserting at the end thereof the following new section: Section 511.9—Swimming Pools. Swimming pools shall be enclosed with an approved fence or other approved barrier with a gate that can be locked.

SIXTEENTH ARTICLE. — To see if the Town will amend the Building Code by striking out sub-paragraphs 3, 4, 5, 6, 7 and 8 of paragraph c of Section 208 of Article 2 of the Building Code and substituting in place thereof, the following sub-paragraph 3:

3. Electrical Fees

    a. New buildings per occupancy or per meter socket $5.00

    b. Alterations per occupancy or per meter socket 2.00

    c. All other work 1.00

    Maximum fee 250.00

SEVENTEENTH ARTICLE. — To see if the Town will appropriate from the Sale of the Lowell Playground Fund the sum of thirty-five thousand dollars ($35,000) to be expended by the Building Commission, with the approval of the Park Commissioners and the Board of Selectmen, for the construction of a field house at Beacon Playground including any furnishings, said appropriation to include the demolition of the present building and to provide for site improvements based on completed plans by Architectural Planning Associates, Architects, dated December 27, 1962.

EIGHTEENTH ARTICLE. — To see if the Town will raise and appropriate the sum of twenty thousand dollars ($20,000) for study of the Town's off-street parking and traffic problems to be conducted by the Planning Board.

NINETEENTH ARTICLE. — To see if the Town will raise and appropriate the sum of thirty-two thousand two hundred dollars ($32,-200) to create a new vehicular crossover of the Beacon Street median opposite Centre Street, widen Webster Street between Beacon Street and the Webster Street Parking Lot, close the existing Beacon Street crossings between Centre Street and Harvard Street, modify the Winchester Street crossing of Beacon Street and signalize both of these intersections.

TWENTIETH ARTICLE. — To see if the Town will authorize the Selectmen to purchase or take by eminent domain under Chapter 79 of the General Laws, for the purpose of the Fire Department, two certain parcels of land on Babcock Street, being shown on the 1962 Assessors' Plan as Lots 12 and 13 in Block 47, and bounded and described as follows:

NORTHWESTERLY by Babcock Street;
NORTHEASTERLY by land now or formerly of Sage Realty, Inc.;
SOUTHEASTERLY by land now or formerly of Young Israel of Brookline, Inc., J. A. Patterson and R. A. and E. Jenning;
SOUTHWESTERLY by land now or formerly of A. and H. D. Haffer,

and will raise and appropriate the sum of thirty-two thousand three hundred and seventy-five dollars ($32,375) to pay for the same or to be paid for land damages or other costs and expenses in connection therewith.

TWENTY-FIRST ARTICLE. — To see if the Town will raise and appropriate the sum of three hundred fifty thousand dollars ($350,000) to be expended by the Building Commission, with the approval of the Board of Selectmen, for the construction of, and for originally equipping and furnishing, a new Fire Station on land of the Town on Babcock Street, authorization for the acquisition of which was given by vote of the Town under the preceding article.

TWENTY-SECOND ARTICLE. — To see if the Town will raise and appropriate, or appropriate from available funds, the sum of eight thousand six hundred and ten dollars ($8,610) for the furnishing and installation of traffic control signalization for the proposed construction of Washington Street, in the Village Area, under the Chapter 90 Program.

TWENTY-THIRD ARTICLE. — To see if the Town will raise and appropriate, or appropriate from available funds in the Treasury, the sum of seventy thousand dollars ($70,000) for the replacement of the present stairs with permanent Portland cement concrete construction and the walks with bituminous concrete with installation of a surface water drain and catch basins in Summit Path, from Beacon Street to Lancaster Terrace and from Lancaster Terrace to York Terrace.

TWENTY-FOURTH ARTICLE. — To see if the Town will raise and appropriate, or appropriate from available funds, the sum of seventy-six thousand nine hundred dollars ($76,900) for the reconstruction and repair of streets under the Chapter 90 Road Program.

TWENTY-FIFTH ARTICLE. — To see if the Town will vote to authorize and instruct the Assessors, with the advice of the Selectmen, to provide by contract for the expert appraisal of all taxable real property in the Town by outside, independent appraisers and for the defense of their appraisal in any appellate proceedings within a period of not less than four years following the completion thereof, and to provide also that the full and fair cash values of all such property as so appraised be reported to the Assessors on or before December 31, 1963, and that such reports be open to public inspection forthwith after the filing of same with the Assessors, and to raise and appropriate for the purposes of this article the sum of one hundred and fifty thousand dollars ($150,000), or will take any other action with respect thereto.

TWENTY-SIXTH ARTICLE. — To see if the Town will amend the By-Laws so as to instruct the Advisory Committee, or a special standing committee, if preferred, to review and report at each Annual Town Meeting, on the progress and action taken under articles voted in Warrants of the previous year or years; and, if the committee so voted by the Town Meeting shall be the Advisory Committee, then the Annual Advisory Committee Report shall include the said review, or if a special committee be voted, the written report will be made in accordance with Article I, Section 4, of the Brookline By-Laws.

TWENTY-SEVENTH ARTICLE. — To see if the Town will request an amendment to its vote of the 10th article in the Warrant of March 21, 1961 that the present Gymnasium Wing (built in 1925, on about 6500 sq. ft. of land) of the John D. Runkle School be excluded at present from demolition plans; and that the Selectmen and the School Committee, jointly with a Committee appointed by the Moderator, make further study of the utilization of said building for the best interests of the Town and report to the Town Meeting in an Article of the next Special Town Meeting or of the next Annual Town Meeting.

TWENTY-EIGHTH ARTICLE. — To see if the Town will amend the Zoning By-Law by including within the M-3.0 district (Apartment House District M-3.0) that part of Block 165, as designated on the 1962 Assessors' Plan, which is now in the M-2.0 district (Apartment House District M-2.0); said area being further described as follows:

SOUTHERLY by Marion Street;
EASTERLY by Park Street;
NORTHERLY and WESTERLY by the division line between the existing M-2.0 district and the existing G-4.0 district (General Business G-4.0);

and will alter the Zoning Map in such manner as to indicate the foregoing; or will amend and adopt said proposed amendment.

TWENTY-NINTH ARTICLE. — To see if the Town will amend the Zoning By-Law by including in the S-7 district (one-family detached dwelling, minimum lot size 7,000 square feet) the lots designated on Page 88 of the 1962 Atlas of the Town of Brookline as Lots 11 through 16 in Block 341, Lots 1 through 8 in Block 342, Lots 1 through 12 in Block 343, Lots 1 through 6 and 12 in Block 344, Lots 9 through 16 in Block 345, all of which is now designated in the Zoning By-Law as T-5 district (one-family detached dwelling, minimum lot size 4,000 square feet; two-family detached dwelling, minimum lot size 5,000 square feet; one-family attached dwelling, minimum lot size 2,250 square feet) as shown on Zoning Map #10 of the Town of Brookline dated April 26, 1962, bearing the signatures of the members of the Planning Board and made part of the Zoning By-Law by Section 3.2 (a) thereof, or will otherwise amend and adopt said proposed amendment.

THIRTIETH ARTICLE. — To see if the Town will amend the Zoning By-Law by including in the M-2.0 district (which district includes multiple unit apartment houses not to exceed a maximum height of 85 feet) the lots designated on Page 123 of the 1962 Atlas of the Town of Brookline as Lots 17 through 21, all in Block 429, all of which is now designated in the Zoning By-Law as T-6 district (which district includes one-family detached dwellings, two-family detached dwellings and one-family attached dwellings) as shown on Zoning Map #10 of the Town of Brookline dated April 26, 1962, bearing the signatures of the members of the Planning Board and made a part of the Zoning By-Law, by Section 3.2 (a) thereof, or will otherwise amend and adopt said proposed amendment.

THIRTY-FIRST ARTICLE. — To see if the Town will amend the Zoning By-Law by adopting the following amendments thereto or will otherwise amend and adopt said proposed amendments, or will take any other action with respect thereto: —

ARTICLE 3

1. To amend Section 3.2 by adding the following paragraph (f) thereto:
    (f) Where a boundary line between districts divides a lot in single owner-ship, all or part of the gross floor area calculated to be permitted on the more restricted part of the lot may be transferred to the less re-stricted part, provided that the aggregate gross floor area on the entire lot does not exceed the sum of the areas calculated to be permitted on

each part thereof, provided that all other dimensional requirements are met as applicable in each district and provided that no part of the lot in the more restricted district is used for any use prohibited in that district, including accessory uses other than landscapped open space.

ARTICLE 4

1. To amend Section 4.12 by striking out the last sentence and by substituting in place thereof the following: "Any application for change in use or structure shall require a special permit from the Board of Appeals as provided in Article 9."

2. To amend Section 4.30 by striking Use 7 and substituting in place thereof the following Use 7:
    7. Lodging house, licensed and unlicensed.
       * Licensed lodging house not permitted in M-O.5 Districts, nor in M or business districts on a lot adjacent to the boundary of an S, SC, or T District, and limited in M-1.0 Districts to not more than 20 lodgers. Special permit required for an unlicensed lodging house.

3. To amend Section 4.30 by striking out Use 8 and substituting in place thereof the following Use 8:
    8. Hotel
       * No hotel building permitted in M-O.5 or M-1.0 Districts, nor in business districts within 50 feet from lots in an S, SC, or T District.

4. To amend Section 4.30 by striking out of Use 11 the words "open to the public or connected with a permitted educational use, and" so that Use 11 shall read as follows:
    11. Library or museum, not conducted as a private gainful business.

5. To amend Use 15 of Section 4.30 to read:
    15. Private day nursery, private nursery school, private kindergarten or other private agency giving day care to children, conducted as a gainful business and providing outdoor play area is at such a distance and so screened from any lot line and from any residential structure on an adjoining lot as to avoid a noise nuisance.

6. To amend Section 4.30 by striking Use 24 and the notations following for permitted use in the districts designated and substituting in place thereof the following:
    24. Non-residential parking garage or parking area, other than Use 23.
       * Municipal parking facilities permitted in any district.

Residence				Business			Industry
S	SC	T	M	L	G	O	I
No*	No*	No*	No*	Yes	Yes	No*	Yes

7. To amend Section 4.30 by inserting in Use 34 the word "or" before the word "providing."

8. To amend Section 4.30 by striking Use 66 and the notations following for permitted use in the districts designated.

ARTICLE 5

1. To amend Section 5.12 by striking out paragraphs (b) and (c) therefrom.

112

2. To amend Section 5.30 as follows:

    (i) by striking from paragraph (a) of Section 5.30 the word "greater" and substituting in place thereof the words "less restrictive" so that said paragraph (a) shall read as follows:

        Where the lot abuts other lots to the rear which are subject to the same or less restrictive height limitations:

    (ii) by striking from paragraph (b) of Section 5.30 the word "lesser" and substituting in place thereof the words "more restrictive" so that said paragraph (b) shall read as follows:

        Where the lot abuts other lots to the rear which are subject to more restrictive height limitations:

    (iii) by adding at the end of paragraph (b) of Section 5.30 the following paragraph (4):

        (4) For a building or buildings on a lot whose frontage is not more than 160 feet but whose depth is greater than 160 feet:

            (i) Height shall be measured from the record grade of the street opposite the midpoint of the street frontage of the lot, or, if a corner lot, of the street frontage having the lower record grade.

            (ii) If the grade of the natural ground contiguous to the building is not more than 10 feet higher than the record grade of the street, height may be measured from the mean grade of said natural ground.

            (iii) If the grade of the natural ground contiguous to the building is more than 10 feet higher than the record grade of the street, height may be measured from a level 10 feet above said record grade.

3. To amend Section 5.40 by striking out said section and substituting in place thereof the following Section 5.40:

SECTION 5.40 — WALLS NOT PARALLEL TO LOT LINES

Where a wall of a building is not parallel with its corresponding lot line, the average width or depth of any yard or setback shall not be less than the dimension specified in Section 5.00 (Table of Dimensional Requirements) for the required width or depth, provided that said yard or setback shall not be narrower at any point than 3/4 of the required width or depth.

4. To amend Section 5.43 by striking out said Section and substituting in place thereof the following Section 5.43: SECTION 5.43 — EXCEPTIONS TO YARD AND SETBACK REQUIREMENTS.

Under a special permit after a hearing, the Board of Appeals may permit, in lieu of the requirements for yards or setbacks specified in this By-Law, the substitution of such other dimensional requirements as shall assure the same standard of amenity to nearby properties as would have been provided by compliance with the regulations of the By-Law.

5. To amend the last sentence of Section 5.51 to read as follows: "In no case shall any such projection come within five feet of any front lot line except in districts where no front yard is required."

6. To amend Section 5.63 to read as follows:

SECTION 5.63 — ACCESSORY BUILDINGS OR STRUCTURES IN SIDE YARDS

In any S, SC, T, or M District no part of any accessory building or structure situated within 75 feet of the street line, or within a distance equal to three-fourths of the lot depth if that be less, shall extend within any required side yard. Elsewhere on the lot such building or structure may extend into the side yard one-half the required width, except as may be permitted in Section 5.44.

7. To amend Section 5.72 by striking out said section and substituting in place thereof the following Section 5.72:

SECTION 5.72 — ACCESSORY BUILDINGS OR STRUCTURES IN REAR YARDS

Accessory buildings or structures may occupy up to 25 per cent of the required rear yard provided that no such accessory building or structure within a required rear yard shall exceed 15 feet in height, nor be located closer to any side lot line than four feet, except as may be permitted in Section 5.44.

8. To amend Article 5 by inserting the following Section 5.74 after Section 5.73 thereof:

SECTION 5.74 — FENCES AND TERRACES IN REAR YARDS

Subject to Section 5.45, the provisions of Section 5.70 shall not apply to fences, hedges or walls not over seven feet high above the natural grade in the required rear yard nor to terraces, steps, uncovered porches, or other similar features not over three feet high above the level of the floor of the ground story.

ARTICLE 6

1. To amend Section 6.00 by striking out paragraph (c) therefrom and by substituting in place thereof the following paragraph (c):

   (c) Where a parking facility is a principal use of any lot, it shall not be opened to use until the Building Commissioner has issued a certificate of compliance to the effect that the lot conforms to the provisions of Section 6.13 or any other conditions specified by the Board of Appeals. Such certificate may be revoked by the Building Commissioner upon violation of any of the conditions set forth in Section 6.13 or by the Board of Appeals.

2. To amend Section 6.11 (a) (2) by inserting the words "in business districts" between the words "uses" and "is" so that said Section 6.11 (a) (2) shall read as follows:

   (2) Off-street parking space shall not be required when the computed requirement for non-residential uses in business districts is six spaces or less.

3. To amend Section 6.13 as follows:

   (a) by adding to paragraph (e) (1) the following:

   ; except for a parking stall the sole access to which is an alley adjacent to rear lot lines and so arranged that there is at least 20 feet of clear backing between the rear line of the parking stall and the opposite and more distant line of the alley.

   (b) by adding to paragraph (e) (2), the following sentence:

   Such setback area shall be landscaped and maintained, subject to Section 5.45.

   (c) by amending paragraph (e) (3) (ii) to read:

   "from the side lot line in the front and side yard, the distance specified for building setback under Article 5, Section 5.00. Such setback area shall be landscaped and maintained subject to Section 5.45; and

114

(d) by adding to paragraph (e) (3) (iii) the following sentence:
Such setback area shall be landscaped and maintained, subject to Section 5.45.

(e) by striking from paragraph (j) the words "the effective date of this By-Law," and substituting in place thereof the following: "July 27, 1962, which conformed to all applicable regulations in effect when established,"

(f) by adding the following paragraph (1) at the end thereof:
(1) Under a special permit after a hearing, the Board of Appeals may permit in lieu of the dimensional requirements of this section, where new parking facilities are being installed to serve structures and land uses in existence or for which building permits had been issued at the date of adoption of this By-Law, the substitution of other dimensional requirements provided such substitution is necessary to permit the installation of some or all of the off-street parking spaces that would be required for a similar new building.

4. To amend Section 6.21 (a) (3) as follows:
(a) by striking out the figure "20" where same appears and substituting in place thereof the figure "12."

ARTICLE 7

1. To amend Section 7.0, paragraph (a) by adding the following subparagraph
(7) thereto:
(7) Other temporary signs in connection with the construction or development of a building or lot, by special permit of the Board of Appeals which shall specify limits on the size and number of signs, and the length of time to be maintained.

ARTICLE 8

1. To amend Section 8.1 (b) by striking out the word "reconstructed" and substituting in place thereof the word "repaired."

THIRTY-SECOND ARTICLE. — To see if the Town, pursuant to the provisions of Section 90A of Chapter 32 of the General Laws, will vote to increase the retirement allowance of any former employee of the Town who was retired on account of injury sustained in the performance of his duty.

THIRTY-THIRD ARTICLE. — To see if the Town will rescind the authority to the Treasurer to borrow two hundred and twenty-five thousand dollars ($225,000) for the purpose of defraying a portion of the development, acquisition and operating costs of the Farm Redevelopment Project in the Town of Brookline and to issue bonds or notes therefor, contained in the second vote adopted under the eighth article at the Annual Town Meeting held on March 29, 1960.

115

THIRTY-FOURTH ARTICLE. — To see if the Town will accept the provisions of Chapter 409 of the Acts of 1962 (General Laws, Chapter 90, Section 18A) entitled, "An Act Authorizing the Commonwealth, the Metropolitan District Commission, and Cities and Towns to Adopt Rules Regulating the Use of Ways by Pedestrians, and Providing for the Non-Criminal Disposition of Violations Thereof."

THIRTY-FIFTH ARTICLE. — To see if the Town will accept the provisions of Section 6-I of Chapter 40 of the General Laws entitled, "An Act Authorizing Certain Cities and Towns to Construct, Reconstruct, Resurface and Repair Certain Private Ways."

THIRTY-SIXTH ARTICLE. — To see if the Town will approve, ratify and confirm the action of the Board of Selectmen in accepting on behalf of the Town, subject to the approval of the Town Meeting, a deed from Martha Pollack and Alvin J. Clark granting an easement to the Town to affix and maintain a plaque on the premises at 83 Beals Street, Brookline, to commemorate the birthplace of John F. Kennedy, President of the U.S.A.; which deed, dated August 18, 1962, was recorded in the Norfolk County Registry of Deeds, Book 4018, Page 173, and is on file with the Town Clerk, or take any other action with respect thereto.

THIRTY-SEVENTH ARTICLE. — To see if the Town will accept the provisions of Chapter 796 of the Acts of 1962 entitled, "An Act Authorizing Cities and Towns to Lease the Space Above Municipal Parking Lots."

THIRTY-EIGHTH ARTICLE. — To see if the Town will raise and appropriate the sum of one hundred and twenty-five thousand dollars ($125,000) to be expended by the Building Commission with the approval of the Board of Selectmen, for the construction of, and for originally equipping and furnishing, an addition to the Incinerator building for the storage and servicing of motor vehicles.

THIRTY-NINTH ARTICLE. — To hear and act upon the reports of Town Officers and Committees.

FORTIETH ARTICLE. — To see if the Town will appropriate from the available funds in the Treasury the sum of one hundred thousand dollars ($100,000) for the purpose of creating a stabilization fund as authorized by General Laws, Chapter 40, Section 5-B.

FORTY-FIRST ARTICLE. — To see if the Town will authorize taking a sum of money voted for the appropriations heretofore made at this meeting and not voted to be borrowed, from any available funds in the treasury, and will authorize the Assessors to use free cash in the treasury in any available funds to that amount in the determination of the 1963 tax rate.

FORTY-SECOND ARTICLE. — To appropriate and raise by borrowing, or to appropriate from other available funds, such sums of money as may be necessary for all or any of the purposes mentioned in the foregoing articles.

Hereof fail not, and make due return of this warrant, with your doings thereon, to the Selectmen seven days at least before the day of said meeting.

Given under our hands at Brookline aforesaid, this eleventh day of February in the year of our Lord one thousand nine hundred and sixty-three.

MATTHEW BROWN
ALAN R. MORSE
LOUISE M. CASTLE
GEORGE F. McNEILLY
GEORGE V. BROWN, Jr.
Board of Selectmen

Appendix C

Caucus Ballot for the Town of Wellesley, Massachusetts
January 15, 1964

MODERATOR
for 1 year
Vote for One

SELECTMAN
for 3 years
Vote for One

TOWN CLERK
for 3 years
Vote for One

TREASURER & COLLECTOR
for 3 years
Vote for One

BOARD OF ASSESSORS
for 3 years
Vote for One

BOARD OF HEALTH
for 3 years
Vote for One

BOARD OF HEALTH
for 1 year
Vote for One

BOARD OF PUBLIC WORKS
for 3 years
Vote for One

HOUSING AUTHORITY
for 5 years
Vote for One

PARK & TREE BOARD
for 3 years
Vote for One

PLANNING BOARD
for 5 years
Vote for One

PLANNING BOARD
for 2 years
Vote for One

RECREATION COMMISSIONERS
for 3 years
Vote for Two

SCHOOL COMMITTEE
for 3 years
Vote for Two

TRUSTEES OF WELLESLEY FREE LIBRARY
for 3 years
Vote for Two

WAR MEMORIAL SCHOLARSHIP FUND TRUSTEE
for 3 years
Vote for One

119

Appendix D

Official Ballot for the Town of Oakham, Massachusetts
Monday, March 2, 1964

To Vote for Candidate Mark a Cross [X] in the Square at the Right of the Name

TOWN CLERK - For Three Years Vote for One	**MODERATOR - For One Year** Vote for One
DOROTHY P. DAY New Braintree Road Candidate for Re-Election Caucus Nominee	FREDERICK H. LANE Scott Road Candidate for Re-Election Nomination Papers
	SAMUEL R. MAXWELL Rutland Road Caucus Nominee
SELECTMAN - For Three Years Vote for One	
SUMNER J. CRAWFORD Lupa Road Nomination Papers	**TAX COLLECTOR - For One Year** Vote for One
LIONEL A. LAJOIE, JR. Old Turnpike Road Caucus Nominee	CATHERINE M. RUSS North Brookfield Road Nomination Papers
	VIRGINIA R. TAYLOR Lupa Road Caucus Nominee
ASSESSOR - For Three Years Vote for One	
LUDWICK SZCZUKA Maple Street Candidate for Re-Election Caucus Nominee	**TRESASURER - For One Year** Vote for One
	RICHARD J. HARDSOG Hunt Road Candidate for Re-Election Caucus Nominee
SCHOOL COMMITTEE - For Three Years Vote for One	
MARY H. PARSONS Maple Street Candidate for Re-Election Caucus Nominee	**AUDITOR - For One Year** Vote for One
	JAMES BARRINGER Georges' Lane Candidate for Re-Election Caucus Nominee
LIBRARY TRUSTEE - For Three Years Vote for One	
DOROTHY V. LUPA North Brookfield Road Candidate for Re-Election Caucus Nominee	**TREE WARDEN - For One Year** Vote for One
	H. ROSCOE CRAWFORD Crawford Road Candidate for Re-Election Caucus Nominee
CEMETERY COMMITTEE - For Three Years Vote for One	
CALVIN C. STEWART Coldbrook Road Caucus Nominee	**CONSTABLE - For One Year** Vote for One
	LUDWICK SZCZUKA Maple Street To fill vacancy Caucus Nominee
PLANNING BOARD - For Five Years Vote for One	
MATILDA M. ANDRESON No. Brookfield Rd. Nomination Papers	**FENCE VIEWERS - For One Year** Vote for Three
STUART T. GLENDYE South Road Caucus Nominee	DONALD C. AGAR Ware Corner Road Candidate for Re-Election Caucus Nominee
	WALTER W. NELSON North Brookfield Road Candidate for Re-Election Caucus Nominee
	VERNO S. TUCKER Lake Dean Candidate for Re-Election Caucus Nominee

Bibliography

Public Documents

Athol, Massachusetts. *Report of the Committee "To Consider the Subject of a Representative Form of Town Government."* Athol: May 15, 1963.

Auburn, Massachusetts. *Report of the Representative Town Meeting Review Committee.* Auburn: January 14, 1963.

Boston, Massachusetts. *Dorchester Town Records.* Fourth Report of the Record Commissioners of the City of Boston. 2nd ed. Boston: Rockwell and Churchill, 1883.

——. *A Report of the Record Commissioners of the City of Boston, Containing the Boston Records from 1700 to 1728.* Boston: Rockwell and Churchill, 1883.

——. *Report of the Town Convention.* Boston: 1804.

——. *Second Report of the Record Commissioners of the City of Boston.* Boston: Rockwell and Churchill, 1877.

——. *Several Rules, Orders, and By-Laws Made and Agreed upon by the Freeholders and Inhabitants of Boston of the Massachusets, at their Meeting May 12, and September 22, 1701.* Boston: Bartholomew Green, 1702.

——. *A Volume of Records Relating to the Early History of Boston Containing Boston Town Records, 1784–1796.* Boston: Municipal Printing Office, 1903.

——. *A Volume of Records Relating to the Early History of Boston Containing Boston Town Records, 1796 to 1813.* Boston: Municipal Printing Office, 1905.

——. *A Volume of Records Relating to the Early History of Boston Containing Boston Town Records, 1814 to 1822.* Boston: Municipal Printing Office, 1906.

Cambridge, Massachusetts. *The Records of the Town of Cambridge (Formerly Newtowne) Massachusetts 1630–1703.* Cambridge: Printed by order of the City Council under direction of the City Clerk, 1901.

Commonwealth of Massachusetts. *The Acts and Resolves of the Province of the Massachusetts Bay.* Vol. I. Boston: Wright and Potter, 1869.

———. *The Acts and Resolves of the Province of the Massachusetts Bay.* Vol. II. Boston: Wright and Potter, 1874.

———. *The Acts and Resolves of the Province of the Massachusetts Bay.* Vol. III. Boston: Wright and Potter, 1878.

———. *Constitution of the Commonwealth of Massachusetts.* Boston: Published by the Secretary of the Commonwealth, 1963.

———. *The Dicennial Census 1965.* Boston: Secretary of the Commonwealth, 1965.

———. *Opinion of the Justices to the House of Representatives.* 347 Mass. 792 (1964).

———. *Report of the Commission to Complete the Work of Revising and Codifying the Laws Relating to Towns.* Senate No. 2, 1920.

———. *Report Submitted by the Legislative Research Council Relative to Town Meetings in Regional Schools.* House of Representatives No. 3687. December 27, 1961.

Framingham, Massachusetts. *Report of the Committee Studying Changes in the Town Government.* Framingham: March, 1965.

Holden, Massachusetts. *Report of the Committee To Study the Representative Form of Town Meeting for Holden.* Holden: No date.

Books and Pamphlets

Adams, Herbert B. *The Germanic Origin of New England Towns.* Baltimore: Johns Hopkins University Studies in Historical and Political Science. Vol. I, No. II, 1882.

———. *Norman Constables in America.* Baltimore: Johns Hopkins University Studies in Historical and Political Science. Vol. I, No. VIII, 1883.

Baylies, Francis. *Historical Memoir of the Colony of New Plymouth.* Vol. I. Boston: Wiggin & Lunt, 1866.

Bolton, Geoffrey. *A Handbook for Town Moderators.* 2d ed. Boston: Massachusetts Federation of Taxpayers Associations, Inc., 1954.

Bridenbaugh, Carl. *Cities in the Wilderness.* New York: The Ronald Press Company, 1938.

Bryce, James. *The American Commonwealth.* 2nd ed. revised, Vol. I. London: Macmillan and Company, 1891.

Chamberlain, Mellen. *A Documentary History of Chelsea: 1624–1824*. Vol. I. Boston: The Massachusetts Historical Society, 1908.

Chandler, Alfred D. *Local Self-Government*. Brookline, Mass.: The Riverdale Press, 1908.

Channing, Edward. *Town and County Government in the English Colonies of North America*. Baltimore: Johns Hopkins University Studies in Historical and Political Science. Vol. X, No. X, 1884.

Committee for Economic Development. *Modernizing Local Government*. New York: Committee for Economic Development, July 1966.

de Tocqueville, Alexis. *Democracy in America*. 3rd American ed. New York: George Adlard, 1839.

De Wolf, Austin. *The Town Meeting: A Manual of Massachusetts Law*. Boston: George B. Reed, 1890.

Drake, Francis S. *The Town of Roxbury*. Boston: Municipal Printing Office, 1905.

Drake, Samuel G. *The History and Antiquities of Boston, from Its Settlement in 1630 to the Year 1770*. Boston: Luther Stevens, 1856.

Fairlie, John A. *Local Government in Counties, Towns and Villages*. New York: The Century Co., 1906.

Guide for Establishing a Representative Town Meeting. Amherst: Bureau of Government Research, University of Massachusetts, 1957.

Haller, William, Jr. *The Puritan Town-Planting in New England Colonial Development 1630–1660*. New York: Columbia University Press, 1951.

Hardy, Henry W. *The Role of the Town Counsel*. Amherst: Bureau of Government Research, University of Massachusetts, 1960.

Haskins, George L. *Law and Authority in Early Massachusetts*. New York: The Macmillan Company, 1960.

Haynes, George H. *Representation and Suffrage in Massachusetts, 1620–1691*. Baltimore: Johns Hopkins University Studies in Historical and Political Science, 1894.

Hosmer, James K. *Samuel Adams: The Man of the Town Meeting*. Baltimore: Johns Hopkins University Studies in Historical and Political Science. Vol. II, No. IV, 1884.

Jackson, W. Eric. *Local Government in England and Wales.* Hardmonsworth, Middlesex: Penguin Books, Ltd., 1959.

Jameson, J. Franklin. (ed.) *Johnson's Wonder-Working Providence: 1628–1651.* New York: Barnes & Noble, Inc., 1952.

Johnson, Richard B., Trustman, Benjamin A., and Wadsworth, Charles Y. *Town Meeting Time.* Boston: Little, Brown and Company, 1962.

Kittredge, Henry C. *Barnstable 1639–1939.* Barnstable, Massachusetts: Tercentenary Committee, 1939.

MacLear, Anne Bush. *Early New England Towns: A Comparative Study of Their Development.* New York: Columbia University, 1908.

Martin, Roscoe C. *Grass Roots.* New York: Harper & Row, Publishers, 1964.

Munro, William B. *The Government of the United States.* 4th ed. New York: The Macmillan Company, 1937.

Notestein, Wallace. *The English People on the Eve of Colonization.* New York: Harper & Row, Publishers, 1954.

Padover, Saul. *The Complete Jefferson.* New York: Sloan and Pearce, 1943.

Paige, Lucius R. *History of Cambridge, Massachusetts: 1630–1877.* Boston: H. O. Houghton and Company, 1877.

Powell, Lyman P. (ed.). *Historic Towns of New England.* New York: G. P. Putnam's Sons, 1899.

Powell, Sumner C. *Puritan Village.* Middletown, Conn.: Wesleyan University Press, 1963.

Shipton, Clifford K. *Roger Conant.* Cambridge: Harvard University Press, 1944.

Shurtleff, Nathaniel B. (ed.) *Records of the Governor and Company of the Massachusetts Bay in New England.* Vol. I. Boston: From the Press of William White, 1853.

———. *Records of the Governor and Company of the Massachusetts Bay in New England.* Vol. II. Boston: From the Press of William White, 1853.

———. *Records of the Colony of New Plymouth in New England.* Boston: From the Press of William White, 1855.

Sly, John F. *Town Government in Massachusetts (1620–1930).* Cambridge: Harvard University Press, 1930.

Tercentenary of the Landing of the Popham Colony at the Mouth of the Kennebec River, August 29, 1907. Portland: Maine Historical Society, 1907.

Usher, Roland G. *The Pilgrims and Their History.* New York: The Macmillan Company, 1918.

Webster, Clarence M. *Town Meeting Country.* New York: Duell, Sloan & Pearce, 1945.

Wertenbaker, Thomas Jefferson. *The Puritan Oligarchy: The Founding of American Civilization.* New York: Charles Scribner's Sons, 1947.

Whitmore, William H. *The Massachusetts Civil List for the Colonial and Provincial Periods: 1630–1774.* Albany: J. Munsell, 1870.

Winthrop, John. *The History of New England from 1630 to 1649.* Boston: Little, Brown and Company, 1853.

Wood, Robert C. *Suburbia: Its People and Their Politics.* Boston: Houghton Mifflin Company, 1959.

Articles

Adams, Charles Francis. "The Genesis of the Massachusetts Town, and the Development of Town Meeting Government," *Proceedings of the Massachusetts Historical Society,* VII (January, 1892), 172-211.

Adlow, Elijah. "Lemuel Shaw and Municipal Corporations," *Massachusetts Law Quarterly,* XLIV (July, 1959), 53-98.

Alexander, John W. and Berger, Morroe, "Is the Town Meeting Finished?" *The American Mercury,* (August, 1959), 144-51.

Chandler, Alfred D. "Remarks of Alfred D. Chandler," *Massachusetts Law Quarterly,* IV (February, 1919), 77-91.

Cunningham, Richard H. "Every Citizen a Legislator; But It Takes Good Citizens," *Worcester Telegram* (Massachusetts), March 5, 1964, p. 6.

————. "Forty Massachusetts Communities Now Use the Representative Town Meeting Idea," *Worcester Telegram* (Massachusetts), March 4, 1964, p. 6.

————. "Representative Town Meetings: The Shrewsbury Experience," *Worcester Telegram* (Massachusetts), March 6, 1959, p. 6.

————. "What's Gone Wrong with the Old Town Meeting?" *Worcester Telegram* (Massachusetts), March 3, 1959, p. 6.

"The Fading Town Meeting," *National Civic Review*, LIV (October, 1965), 464-65 and 522.

Howes, Rev. Robert G. Letter to the Editor, *The Massachusetts Selectman*, XIX (October, 1960), 34-35.

Knowles, Howard S. "How Massachusetts Towns Choose Their Officers," *Sunday Telegram* (Worcester, Massachusetts), February 12, 1961, p. B-1.

Long, John A. "N. E. Town Fights for Landscape," *The Christian Science Monitor*, February 13, 1965, p. 2.

Lord, Arthur. "The Representative Town Meeting in Massachusetts," *Massachusetts Law Quarterly*, IV (February, 1919), 49-74.

Parker, Joel. "The Origin, Organization, and Influence of the Towns of New England," *Proceedings of the Massachusetts Historical Society*, IX (1866-1867), 14-65.

Peairs, C. A. "Introduction," *Boston University Law Review*, XXXVIII (Summer, 1958), 339-46.

Robbins, L. H. "Democracy, Town Meeting Style," *The New York Times Magazine*, March 23, 1947, pp. 24, 35, and 38.

Smith, Louis H. Letter to the Editor, *The Massachusetts Selectman*, XX (January, 1961), 18.

Tilden, Robert J. "Separation of Powers and the Representative Town Meeting," *Massachusetts Law Quarterly*, XLII (March, 1957), 24-28.

———. "Some Fundamentals of Town Meetings," *Massachusetts Law Quarterly*, XLVII (June, 1962), 165-74.

———. "Town Government," *Boston University Law Review*, XXXVIII (Summer, 1958), 347-89.

Zimmerman, Joseph F. "Genesis of the Massachusetts Town," *Social Science*, XLI (April, 1966), 76-83.

———. "On the Other Hand," *National Civic Review*, LV (January, 1966), 14-20.

———. "The Open Town Meeting: A Tenacious Institution," *Civic Affairs*, XIII (October, 1965), 16-19.

———. "Representative Town Meeting," *The Massachusetts Selectman*, XXV (April, 1966), 7-8, 10, and 30.

———. "Representative Town Meeting: An Evaluation," *The Massachusetts Selectman*, XXV (July, 1966), 17-18.

Unpublished Material

Leiffer, Donald B. "Town Manager Government in Massachusetts." Unpublished Ph.D. dissertation, Harvard University, 1939.

Melick, Richard P. "Memo To Town Meeting Members." Natick, Massachusetts, March 8, 1953 (Mimeographed).

"Model By-Laws for Massachusetts Towns." Boston: Massachusetts Federation of Taxpayers Associations, Inc., 1940 (Mimeographed).

"Representative Town Meetings in Massachusetts." Boston: Massachusetts Federation of Taxpayers Associations, Inc., June, 1945 (Mimeographed).

General Index

GENERAL INDEX

Absentee voting, 23-24
Accidental Representation, 57
Acton, 39
Adams, 19, 60
Adams, Herbert B., 13
Adams, Samuel, 52
Adams v. *Cook*, 35
Ad hoc citizens committees, 42
Advisory opinion, 65
Agawam, 22, 24, 61, 64, 66
Amesbury, 26, 56
Amherst, 60-61, 70
Anglo-Saxon institutions, 12-13
Annual report, 19-20, 47
Annual town meeting, 15-48
  annual report, 19-20, 47
  by-laws, 46-48
  conduct of business, 28-44
  election of town officials, 20-27
  Mr. Moderator, 30-35
  quorum requirement, 38-40
  recall, 27-28
  role of factions, 42-44
  role of finance committee, 37
  role of pressure groups, 41-42
  role of select committees, 40-41
  role of town clerk, 35-36
  role of town counsel, 36-37
  warrant, 16-19
Arlington, 27, 58, 66
Ashburnham, 15
Ashland, 56, 87
Assessors, 21, 52
Assistant moderator, 31
Associated Fire Fighters of
  Massachusetts, AFL-CIO, 68
Athol, 37, 56-57, 61-62, 84
Attorney General of the Common-
  wealth, 15, 18, 34, 36, 46
Auburn, 26, 57, 61, 64
Auburn Representative Town Meeting
  Review Committee, 64
Auditors, 21
Auditors of account, 52
Avon, 25

Barnstable, 39
Belchertown, 24
Belmont, 62, 64, 67
Berlin, 19-20, 34
Blomquist v. *Arlington,* 34 fn, 66 fn
Blue collar workers, 43
Board of health, 21
Board of public welfare, 21

Board of registrars, 23
Boston, 7, 51-55
Boston Edison Company, 42
Boston Records, 7fn, 10, 11fn, 12
Boxboro, 42
Boxboro Businessmen's Associa-
  tion, 42
Boylston, 25, 40
Braintree, 27
Brookline, 26, 55-56, 58, 67, 82
Brown v. *Town of Carlisle,* 46fn
Bryce, James, 76, 78
By-Laws, 18, 22, 30-31, 33, 35, 37-38,
  44, 46-48, 53-54, 58-59, 61, 66, 69

Cambridge, 7, 10
Cambridge Records, 7fn, 10
Candidate for re-election, 59
Canton, 24-25
Cape Ann, 3
Carpetbaggers, 43
Caucus, 22-23
Chamber of Commerce, 26
Chance representation, 57
Chandler, Alfred D., 55-56
Charlestown, 10, 14
Charlton, 10
Charter commission, 58
Checkers, 38
Checklist, 44
Chester, 39
Churchwardens, 13-14
Citizen apathy, 55, 63, 77, 84
Citizen associations, 25-26
Citizen committees, 40-41
Citizen education, 87
Citizen participation, 79
City charter, 55, 87
City council, 75, 87-89
City government, 53-54, 88-89
Clerks of the market, 20
Clinton, 24
Cliques, 42-44
Code of ethics, 63, 66
Collectors of taxes, 21, 52
Commission to Complete the Work of
  Revising and Codifying the Laws
  Relating to Towns, 46fn
Commissioner for assessments, 20
Committee for Economic Develop-
  ment, 75, 81fn
Committee Studying Changes in the
  Town Government, 85fn
Commonage, 9

133

134

135

137